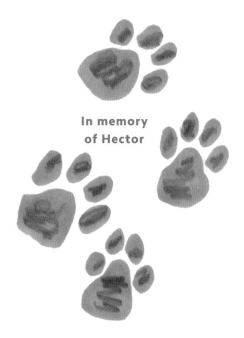

In memory
of Hector

WOOLLY WOOFERS

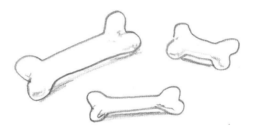

DEBBIE BLISS

Illustrations by Jo Clark

Photographs by Richard Burns

LARK
New York

CONTENTS

INTRODUCTION

I love dogs. This lifelong love affair began when I was six years old and Kim, a ball of black-and-white fluff, was placed on my lap while I was in bed recovering from the flu. Since that day, there have been very few times in my life when I have been without a dog. There was Dick, a crossbreed who planned his escapes with the thoroughness of Houdini. Sometimes on my way to work, even though every exit had been blocked off, I would see a familiar upturned bottom in a dustbin and, using my coat belt as a leash, retrace my steps back home with the runaway. After Dick came Hector, a Heinz-57 variety mongrel who, unless shorn regularly, developed impressive dreadlocks. Hector's eagerness to please was immensely touching. Everyone who came to the door was greeted by Hector, an ambulant fur ball with a gift firmly gripped between his teeth—perhaps a pen, sometimes a ball of yarn, and just occasionally an item of underwear.

Which brings me to the major, very selfish, reason why I love dogs: they love us. I am not interested in a snooty pet who can take you or leave you (fellow dog lovers, you know who I mean). I want unconditional love. I want a pet who, when you pop out to the kitchen for a few minutes, will behave as though you had been gone for months on your return. Whenever other pet owners try to persuade me that their animals are affectionate, they describe them to me as "Just like a dog, honestly." I remain unconvinced.

Now I have two dogs, Monty the beagle and Smiffy the Parson Russell Terrier. The former is obsessed by food and the latter by his devotion to the Bliss family… and the chasing of squirrels. Like a parent who gets broody when their last child goes off to school, I am now beginning to wonder how I might

smuggle a third dog past my husband.

This book combines two of my great loves; knitting and dogs. It was important to me that this knitwear collection included projects that are a lot of fun as well as a little bit silly, the Cow Bow-Wow and the Wolf in Sheep's Clothing, for example. However, to counterbalance the designs that are comic or cute, there is a selection of more classic dog coats. After all, the dog is a noble beast and so it is important that his or her apparel should be appropriately dignified, such as the traditional tartan coat for a Highland Hound or the handsome tweed cape for Sherlock Bones.

I have authored many knitting books over the years but I can truly say that I have never had quite as much fun as on the photo shoots for this book. The dog owners were as fascinating as their pets; I loved the way that the men in particular beamed with pride when their pets went through their paces and the relief that all of us masters or mistresses felt when our pooches didn't let us down. Smiffy failed miserably to set the bar by continually wandering off from his "mark," distracted by a fly, a rustle of paper, or simply nothing at all. We will never know whether Monty would have made the grade as unfortunately an operation on his legs meant his modeling days had to be temporarily suspended.

My favorite knitting-related photograph is one where I am working on a sweater with Monty resting his head on my lap and Smiffy draped across my neck along the back of the sofa. Surely all doggy devotion should be rewarded with the best possible wardrobe, lovingly knitted by their owner.

Debbie Bliss

KNITTING FOR DOGS

While we were photographing the dog models featured throughout this book, one thing became very clear: whether large or small, dogs come in very different shapes and sizes. A small dog can be stocky with a thick neck, while a large dog can be literally whippet thin. To determine which style of coat might suit the shape of your dog best, first measure the length of their back and the circumference of their chest and compare these measurements to those given for each knitted design. This will give you the basic size to follow when knitting your dog's coat, however it is not an exact science because your dog's musculature, neck size, and whether they are smooth or wire coated all come into the equation.

For the first coat you knit—let's be honest, your dog is going to need more than one outfit—I recommend that you play it safe and start with the most versatile style, the simple coat with straps, such as the Pirate Pooch (page 42), the Give-A-Dog-A-Bone Coat (page 82), or the Highland Hound (page 94). As the neck and chest straps can easily be altered, this style of coat can be adjusted to fit every shape and size or dog. If there is a motif that you particularly like from another style of coat, perhaps the bullseye on the Mod Dog coat (page 36) or the number one on the Scrum Hound sweater (page 106), then feel free to mix and match the style of coat and motif. Just make sure that you position the motif centrally on the back panel of the coat.

Once you progress on to the other styles of coat, most of the designs can be adjusted by adding a few extra stitches and additional rows to enlarge the length or width.

The next page has useful descriptions of the different styles of dog coat included in this book.

SIMPLE COAT WITH STRAPS

Easy-to-adjust straight back panel with neck and chest straps. Suits all body shapes.

Pirate Pooch (page 42)
Give-A-Dog-A-Bone Coat
 (page 82)
Clan Canine (page 86)
Highland Hound (page 94)
Santa's Little Helper (page 136)

"TUBE" COAT WITH WIDE NECK

A cylindrical tube with legholes and a wide neck opening. Suits dogs with broad necks, such as pugs and French bulldogs.

Aran Doggy (page 14)
Good-Boy Gansey (page 100)

SIMPLE COAT WITH FRONT GUSSET

A straight back panel with a triangular front gusset. Suits small-chested dogs, such as Yorkshire terriers, miniature dachshunds, and most puppies.

Puppy Love (page 20)
Man's Bee Friend (page 76)

"TUBE" COAT WITH GARTER EDGE NECK

A cylindrical tube with legholes and a garter edge around the neck opening. Suits dogs with "furry" necks such, as Scotties, springer spaniels, miniature schnauzers as well as dogs with wide necks, such as French bulldogs.

Sherlock Bones (page 24)
Wolf in Sheep's Clothing
 (page 30)
Le Chien à la Mode (page 48)
Fair Isle Furbaby (page 112)
Parka Barker (page 118)

VEST WITH BACK FASTENING

A button-back vest with legholes and a wide neck opening. Suits most body shapes.

Deputy Dog (page 124)

"TUBE" COAT WITH RIB NECK

A cylindrical tube with legholes and a close-fitting rib around the neck opening. Suits most body shapes.

Mod Dog (page 36)
Cow Bow-Wow (page 66)
Mardi Gras Mutt (page 72)
Scrum Hound (page 106)

TYPES OF YARNS

The yarns I have chosen for the designs in this book range from my Rialto 4ply fine merino wool to my chunkier yarns, each with their own unique qualities that contribute to the designs. A yarn may create crisp stitch detail in a simple pattern, such as on the Sherlock Bones coat (page 24) worked in Luxury Tweed Aran, or provide a soft drape, such as on the Pierrot Ruff (page 130) knitted with Rialto 4ply.

Unless you are using up your stash to make the smaller items in this book, do make the effort to buy the yarn stated in the pattern. Each of these designs has been created with a specific yarn in mind. A different yarn may not produce the same quality of fabric or have the same wash-and-wear properties. From an aesthetic point of view, the clarity of a subtle stitch pattern may be lost if a project is knitted in an inferior yarn. However, there may be occasions when a knitter needs to substitute a yarn and so the following is a guide to making the most informed choices.

Always buy a yarn that is the same weight as the one used in the pattern and check that the gauge of both yarns is the same. Where you are substituting a different fiber, be aware of the design. A cable pattern designed for cotton when knitted in wool will pull in because of the greater elasticity of the yarn and will alter the proportions of the knitting.

Check the length of the ball of yarn. Yarns that weigh the same can be different lengths, so you may need to buy more or fewer balls.

The following are a guide to the weights and types of the yarns used in this book.

DEBBIE BLISS BABY CASHMERINO
- A fine-weight yarn
- 55% wool, 33% microfiber, 12% cashmere
- Approx 136yd (125m) per 1¾oz (50g) ball

DEBBIE BLISS BLUE FACED LEICESTER ARAN
- An Aran-weight yarn
- 100% wool
- Approx 82yd (75m) per 1¾oz (50g) ball

DEBBIE BLISS CASHMERINO ARAN
- An Aran-weight yarn
- 55% wool, 33% microfiber, 12% cashmere
- Approx 98yd (90m) per 1¾oz (50g) ball

DEBBIE BLISS LUXURY TWEED ARAN
- An Aran-weight yarn
- 90% wool, 10% angora
- Approx 96yd (88m) per 1¾oz (50g) ball

DEBBIE BLISS MIA
- A double-knitting-weight yarn
- 50% cotton, 50% wool
- Approx 109yd (100m) per 1¾oz (50g) ball

DEBBIE BLISS RIALTO 4PLY
- A super-fine-weight yarn
- 100% extra fine merino wool
- Approx 196yd (180m) per 1¾oz (50g) ball

DEBBIE BLISS RIALTO CHUNKY
- A chunky-weight yarn
- 100% merino wool
- Approx 65yd (60m) per 1¾oz (50g) ball

DEBBIE BLISS RIALTO DK
- A double-knitting-weight yarn
- 100% merino wool
- Approx 115yd (105m) per 1¾oz (50g) ball

DEBBIE BLISS ROMA
- A bulky-weight yarn
- 70% wool, 30% alpaca
- Approx 87yd (80m) per 3½oz (100g) ball

LOUISA HARDING LUZIA
- A super-bulky-weight furry yarn
- 80% viscose, 20% nylon
- Approx 43yd (40m) per 1¾oz (50g) ball

BUYING YARN

The label on the yarn will carry all the essential information you need as to gauge, needle size, weight, and yardage. Importantly it will also have the dye lot. Yarns are dyed in batches or lots, which can vary considerably. Your retailer may not have the same dye lot later on, so buy all your yarn for a project at the same time. If you know that sometimes you use more yarn than the amount quoted in the pattern, buy extra. If it is not possible to buy all the yarn you need with the same dye lot, use the different ones where it may not show as much, on a neck or border, as a change of dye lot across a main piece will be more visible.

At the time of buying the yarn, check the pattern to ensure you already have the needles you require. If not, buy them now, as it will save a lot of frustration when you get home.

SAFETY TIPS

While you are knitting, keep all balls of yarn out of reach from your pets. Strands of yarn can cause dogs terrible health problems if swallowed, so make sure that you pack away your knitting supplies when they are not in use.

You may only use small amounts of yarn for some of the projects included in this book, but if you substitute the recommended yarn with another it is essential that you choose a comparable good-quality fiber. This is not only to ensure that the coat will be comfortable for your dog to wear but will also keep them safe. Do not substitute yarns with fluffy or hairy fibers, such as mohair, as these fibers can be ingested when licked.

When substituting yarns it is a good idea to check that your yarn choice is machine washable—it makes life that little bit easier to be able to pop a dirty dog coat into the washing machine.

KNITTING ABBREVIATIONS

The standard abbreviations below are used throughout this book. Any abbreviations more specific to a particular design are given at the start of the individual pattern.

approx approximate
beg begin(ning)
cont continu(e)(ing)
cm centimeter(s)
dec decreas(e)(ing)
foll following
g gram(s)
" inch(es)
inc increas(e)(ing)
k knit
kfb knit into front and back of next stitch
M1 make one stitch by picking up the loop lying between the stitch just worked and the next stitch and working into the back of it
m meter(s)
mm millimeter(s)
oz ounce(s)
p purl
patt pattern; work in pattern
psso pass slipped stitch over
rem remain(s)(ing)
rep repeat(ing)
skp slip 1, knit 1, pass slipped stitch over
sl slip
st(s) stitch(es)
St st stockinette stitch
tbl through back loop
tog together
yd yard(s)
yo yarn over right needle to make a new stitch

ARAN
DOGGY

ARAN DOGGY

Whatever the weather, every sea dog needs a traditional fisherman's Aran sweater to protect him from the elements. With its rope-like cables, this rugged hand knit will keep a dog snug whether out on the high seas or back on land.

SIZES

Two sizes small/medium (medium/large)—see coat measurements below and pages 8 and 9 to determine which size suits your dog

Measurements of knitted coat

Length measured along back 18(21)"/46(53.5)cm

Width measured around chest 18¾(20½)"/48(52)cm

MATERIALS

5(6) x 1¾oz (50g) balls of Debbie Bliss Blue Faced Leicester Aran
(100% wool, aran-weight) in ecru

approx 410(492)yd/375(450)m

Pair each of sizes 6, 7, and 8 (4mm, 4.5mm, and 5mm) knitting needles

Set of four size 7 (4.5mm) double-pointed knitting needles

Cable needle

GAUGE

18 sts and 24 rows to 4"/10cm square over St st using size 8 (5mm) needles.

ABBREVIATIONS

C4(6)F slip next 2(3) sts onto cable needle and hold to front of work,
k2(3), then k2(3) from cable needle.

C4(6)B slip next 2(3) sts onto cable needle and hold at back of work,
k2(3), then k2(3) from cable needle.

Tw2R k into the front of 2nd st on left-hand needle, then into the
back of the first st and slip both sts off the needle together.

Also see page 13.

BACK

With size 8 (5mm) needles, cast on 66(70) sts.

Rib row [K1, p1] to end.

Rep the last row 11 more times to complete the collar.

Change to size 6 (4mm) needles.

Rib 12 more rows.

Change to size 8 (5mm) needles.

Now work in patt as follows:

1st row (right side) P2(4), Tw2R, p2, k9, p2, Tw2R, p2, k24, p2, Tw2R, p2, k9, p2, Tw2R, p2(4).

2nd row P to end.

3rd row P2(4), Tw2R, p2, k3, C6F, p2, Tw2R, p2, [C4B, C4F] 3 times, p2, Tw2R, p2, k3, C6F, p2, Tw2R, p2(4).

4th row P to end.

5th and 6th rows Rep 1st and 2nd rows.

7th row P2(4), Tw2R, p2, C6B, k3, p2, Tw2R, p2, [C4F, C4B] 3 times, p2, Tw2R, p2, C6B, k3, p2, Tw2R, p2(4).

8th row Rep 2nd row.

These 8 rows form the patt and are repeated.

Cont in patt until Back measures 15¾(18)"/ 40(46)cm from cast-on edge, ending with a wrong-side row.

SHAPE LOWER BACK

Keeping the patt correct, cont as follows:

Next row Skp, patt to last 2 sts, k2tog.

Next row P to end.

Rep the last 2 rows 3(5) times more. *58 sts.*

Leave these sts on a holder.

FRONT

Work as given for Back until Front measures 7½"/19cm from cast-on edge, ending with a wrong-side row.

SHAPE FOR LEGHOLES

Keeping the patt correct, work as follows:

Bind off 14(15) sts at beg of next 2 rows. *38(40) sts.*

Work 20(22) rows more in patt.

Cast on 14(15) sts at beg of next 2 rows. *66(70) sts.*

Work even in patt until 16 rows fewer have been worked than on Back to lower back shaping, so ending with a wrong-side row.

SHAPE LOWER EDGE

Next row (right side) Patt 18, turn and work on these sts only for first side of shaping, leaving rem 48(52) sts on a spare needle.

Dec one st at inside edge on next 15 rows. *3 sts.*

Bind off.

With right side facing, return to sts on spare needle, slip center 30(34) sts onto a holder, rejoin yarn, patt to end. *18 sts.*

Dec one st at inside edge on next 15 rows. *3 sts.*

Bind off.

LOWER EDGING

Sew right side seam (from cast-on edges to beginning of lower back shaping), leaving leghole edge open.

With right side facing and size 7 (4.5mm) needles, pick up and k 16 sts down left front shaped edge; work k2, [k2tog, k2] 7(8) times across 30(34) sts at center front; pick up and k 16 sts up right front shaped edge, 6(9) sts up shaped edge of back; work k4, [k2tog, k2] 12 times, k2tog, k4 across 58 sts at lower back; then pick up and k 6(10) sts down shaped edge of back. *112(122) sts.*

Rib row [K1, p1] to end.

Rep the last row 5 times more.

Bind off in rib.

LEGHOLE EDGINGS

Sew left side seam, leaving leghole edge open.

With right side facing and size 7 (4.5mm) double-pointed needles, pick up and k 52(64) sts around leghole edge.

Arrange sts over three of the needles.

Rib round [K1, p1] to end.

Rib 4 rounds more.

Bind off in rib.

PUPPY LOVE

*"Happiness is a warm puppy," wrote Peanuts creator Charles M. Schulz.
This over-sized rib turtleneck sweater will keep all young dogs and miniature
breeds cozy and snug.*

SIZE

One size to fit puppies or toy breeds—see coat measurements below and
pages 8 and 9 to determine if this size suits your dog

Measurements of knitted coat

Length measured along back (from top of neck rib when folded over) 13¾"/35cm

Width measured around chest 15¾"/40cm

MATERIALS

One 3½oz (100g) ball Debbie Bliss Roma (70% wool, 30% alpaca; bulky-weight) in lilac

Pair of size 17 (12mm) knitting needles

Size 15 (10mm) circular knitting needle, 15¾"/40cm long

GAUGE

9 sts and 12 rows to 4"/10cm square over St st using size 17 (12mm) needles.

ABBREVIATIONS

See page 13.

COAT WORKED ALL IN ONE

With size 17 (12mm) needles, cast on 23 sts.

BACK

1st row (right side) K2, [k1, p1] to last 3 sts, k3.

2nd row K2, [p1, k1] to last 3 sts, p1, k2.

Rep the last 2 rows once more.

Next row (right side) Knit.

Next row K2, p to last 2 sts, k2.

Rep the last 2 rows until Back measures 6¼"/16cm from cast-on edge, ending with a wrong-side row.

SHAPE FOR FRONT

Next row (right side) Cast on 15 sts, work K1, [p1, k1] 7 times over these 15 cast-on sts, k to end. *38 sts.*

Next row K2, p19, k2, rib to end.

Rep the last 2 rows, then the right side row once more.

Next row (right side) Rib 15 sts, place these sts on a holder, k to end.

Cont to work 9 rows more in patt on rem 23 sts, so ending with a wrong-side row.

Leave sts on a spare needle.

FRONT GUSSET

With wrong side facing, rejoin yarn to 15 sts on holder, rib to end.

Next row (right side) K2, skp, k to last 2 sts, k2tog.

Next row K2, p to last 2 sts, k2.

Rep the last 2 rows until 7 sts rem, ending with a wrong-side row.

NECK RIBBING

Joining row With right side facing and size 15 (10mm) circular needle, k across all sts. *30 sts.*

Work in rounds of rib until ribbing measures 5"/13cm.

Cast off in rib.

SHERLOCK BONES

When contemplating those two-bone problems, a world-renowned canine detective simply must slip on the classic sleuthing outfit of tweed cape coat and matching deerstalker hat. Elementary.

SIZES

Two sizes small (medium)—see coat measurements below and pages 8 and 9 to determine which size suits your dog

Measurements of knitted coat

Length measured along back 12½(15¾)in/32(40)cm

Width measured around chest 19½(26½)in/49(67)cm

Note: Measurements given in the instructions are adjustable depending on your dog.

MATERIALS

For the cape coat

3(4) x 1¾oz (50g) balls of Debbie Bliss Luxury Tweed Aran (90% wool, 10% angora; aran-weight) in bronze approx 288(384)yd/264(352)m

Pair each of sizes 7 and 8 (4.5mm and 5mm) knitting needles

Set of four size 7 (4.5mm) double-pointed knitting needles

For the deerstalker hat

One 1¾oz (50g) ball of Debbie Bliss Luxury Tweed Aran (90% wool, 10% angora; aran-weight) in bronze approx 96yd/88m

Pair of size 7 (4.5mm) knitting needles

Size 7 (4.5mm) crochet hook

Small amount of cotton tartan fabric, for lining, and matching sewing thread

Length of black shirring elastic

Eight small buttons to decorate

GAUGE

18 sts and 24 rows to 4"/10cm square over St st on size 8 (5mm) needles.

ABBREVIATIONS

See page 13.

BACK OF COAT

With size 7 (4.5mm) needles, cast on 44(60) sts.

K 3 rows.

Change to size 8 (5mm) needles.

Next row (right side) K to end.

Next row K3, p to last 3 sts, k3.

Rep the last 2 rows 7 times more.

Beg with a k row, work in St st until Back measures 12½(15¾)"/32(40)cm from cast-on edge, ending with a p row.

Bind off.

FRONT OF COAT

With size 7 (4.5mm) needles, cast on 44(60) sts.

K 3 rows.

Change to size 8 (5mm) needles.

Next row (right side) K to end.

Next row P20(28), k4, p20(28).

Rep the last 2 rows until Front measures 2¾(3½)"/7(9)cm from cast-on edge, ending with a wrong-side row.

SHAPE FOR LEGHOLES

Cont to work in patt as set, bind off 9(11) sts at beg of next 2 rows. *26(38) sts.*

Work 20 rows more.

Cast on 9(11) sts at beg of next 2 rows. *44(60) sts.*

Cont in patt until Front measures 10¼(12½)"/26(32)cm from cast-on edge, ending with a wrong-side row. Bind off.

LEGHOLE EDGINGS

Sew lower side edges of Front to Back with cast-on edge of Front aligned with top of garter st edges of Back. Then leaving the leghole edge open, sew upper side edges of Front to Back, with bound-off edges lined up.

With right side facing and size 7 (4.5mm) double-pointed needles, pick up and k 42(48) sts around leghole edge.

Arrange sts over three of the needles.

1st round P to end.

2nd round K to end.

These 2 rounds form garter st and are repeated once more.

Bind off purlwise.

CAPE AND COLLAR

With size 7 (4.5mm) needles, cast on 85(102) sts.

CAPE

K 5 rows.

1st row (right side) K to end.

2nd row K2, p to last 2 sts, k2.

Rep the last 2 rows 9(12) times more.

Dec row K7, [sl 1, k2tog, psso, k14] 4(5) times, sl 1, k2tog, psso, k7. *75(90) sts.*

Work even in patt for 11 rows.

Dec row K6, [sl 1, k2tog, psso, k12] 4(5) times, sl 1, k2tog, psso, k6. *65(78) sts.*

Work 10 rows, ending with a k row.

COLLAR

The collar is folded back over the cape so the

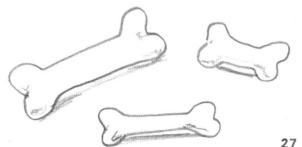

next row becomes the right side of the collar.

Next row (right side of collar) Cast on 8(10) sts, k to end.

Next row Cast on 8(10) sts, k2, p to last 2 sts, k2. *81(98) sts.*

Next 2 rows K to last 30 sts, turn, p to last 30 sts, turn.

Next 2 rows K to last 20 sts, turn, p to last 20 sts, turn.

Next 2 rows K to last 10 sts, turn, p to last 10 sts, turn.

Next row K to end.

Next row K2, p to last 2 sts, k2.

Next row K9(2), [M1, k8] to end. *90(110) sts.*

Next row K2, p to last 2 sts, k2.

Next row K to end.

Rep the last 2 rows 4(6) times more.

K 2 rows. Bind off.

TO FINISH COAT

Fold Collar down onto right side of Cape, and beginning and ending at each side of center front garter st band, sew cast-on edge of Collar and first row of Collar along fold to bound-off edge of Back and Front.

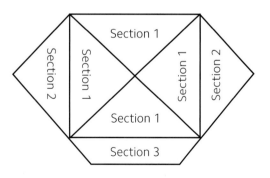

HAT CROWN MAKE 4
SECTION 1 ON DIAGRAM

With size 7 (4.5mm) needles, cast on 16 sts.

K 2 rows.

Beg with a k row, work 14 rows in St st.

Next row K1, k2tog, k to last 3 sts, skp, k1.

Next row P to end.

Rep the last 2 rows until 4 sts rem, ending with a p row.

Next row K1, k2tog, k1.

Next row P to end.

Next row K3tog and bind off.

HAT LINING

Lay a Hat Crown triangle on the lining fabric and cut around the edge, adding 5mm/¼" extra all around for the seams. Cut three more fabric triangles the same size.

Sew the row-end edges of each of the four knitted triangles together to form the crown (see diagram).

Sew the four pieces of lining together as for the knitted pieces.

EARFLAPS MAKE 2
SECTION 2 ON DIAGRAM

With right side facing and size 7 (4.5mm) needles, pick up and k 16 sts along the cast-on edge of one of the sections of the Hat Crown.

Beg with a p row, work 5 rows in St st.

Next row K1, k2tog, k to last 3 sts, skp, k1.

Next row P to end.

Rep the last 2 rows until 4 sts rem, ending with a p row.

Next row K1, k2tog, k1.

Next row P to end.

Next row K3tog and bind off.

Work 2nd earflap to match on opposite side of hat.

HAT PEAK MAKE 1
SECTION 3 ON DIAGRAM

With right side facing and size 7 (4.5mm) needles, pick up and k 16 sts along one cast-on edge between earflaps.

Beg with a p row, work 5 rows in St st.

Next row K1, k2tog, k to last 3 sts, skp, k1.

Next row P to end.

Rep the last 2 rows until 6 sts rem, ending with a p row.
Bind off.

TO FINISH HAT

With 4.5mm (US 7) crochet hook, work a row of single crochet around the outer edges of the hat.

Work a 9"/23cm crochet chain on the tip of each ear flap.

Insert the lining into the crown and sew in place.

Attach a length of shirring elastic to the hat to keep it in place on your dog's head.

Sew eight buttons, equally spaced, onto the central garter st band of the Coat Front.

WOLF IN SHEEP'S CLOTHING

WOLF IN SHEEP'S CLOTHING

This wooly disguise is the perfect lamb-ouflage for when a dog wants to mingle unnoticed with the flock. Just be careful not to baaa-rk as that might give the game away.

SIZES

Two sizes small (medium)—see coat measurements below and pages 8 and 9 to determine which size suits your dog

Measurements of knitted coat

Length measured along back 13½(15)"/34(38)cm

Width measured around chest 16½(19)"/42(48)cm

MATERIALS

2(3) x 1¾oz (50g) balls of Debbie Bliss Blue Faced Leicester Aran (100% wool, aran-weight) in ecru (A) approx 164(246)yd/150(225)m and one 1¾oz (50g) ball in black (B) approx 82yd/75m

Pair of size 8 (5mm) knitting needles

Set of four size 7 (4.5mm) double-pointed knitting needles

GAUGE

24 sts and 27 rows to 4"/10cm square over patt using size 8 (5mm) needles.

BACK OF COAT

With size 8 (5mm) needles and A, cast on 50(58) sts.

1st seed st row [K1, p1] to end.

2nd seed st row [P1, k1] to end.

Rep the last 2 rows once more.

1st row (right side) K1, p to last st, k1.

2nd row K1, * [k1, p1, k1] into next st, p3tog; rep from * to last st, k1.

3rd row K1, p to last st, k1.

4th row K1, * P3tog, [k1, p1, k1] into next st; rep from * to last st, k1.

These 4 rows form the blackberry st patt and are repeated throughout.

Cont in patt until back measures 13(14½)"/ 33(37)cm from cast-on edge, ending with a 3rd patt row.

Dec row (wrong side) K1, [p3tog, p1] to last st, k1.

Bind off rem 26(30) sts.

FRONT OF COAT

Work as given for Back until Front measures 3½(4¼)"/9(11)cm from cast-on edge, ending with a wrong-side row.

SHAPE FOR LEGHOLES

Bind off 8 sts at beg of next 2 rows and 4 sts at beg of foll 2 rows. *26(34) sts.*

Keeping patt correct with a k st at beg and end of each row, work 10(12) rows.

Cast on 4 sts at beg of next 2 rows and 8 sts at beg of foll 2 rows. *50(58) sts.*

Cont in blackberry st patt until Front measures 9¾(11¾)"/25(30)cm from cast-on edge ending with a 3rd patt row.

Dec row (wrong side) K1, [p3tog, p1] to last st, k1.

Bind off rem 26(30) sts.

LEGHOLE EDGINGS

Sew side seams, leaving leghole edges open.

With right side facing, size 7 (4.5mm) double-pointed needles and B, pick up and k 44(48) sts around leghole edge.

Arrange sts over three of the needles.

Rib round [K2, p2] to end.

Rep this round until rib measures 1½"/4cm.

Bind off in rib.

HEAD

With size 7 (4.5mm) double-pointed needles and B, cast on 68(76) sts.

Arrange sts over three of the needles, being careful not to twist the cast-on edge.

Work 21 rounds in k2, p2 rib.

SHAPE FOR FACE

Next round With front facing, k2, [p2, k2] 2(3) times, bind off next 14 sts in rib, rib to end. *54(62) sts.*

Working backward and forward on two needles, cont in k2, p2 rib until face opening measures 2¼"/6cm, ending with a wrong-side row.

With front facing, cast on 14 sts. *68(76) sts.*

Re-arrange sts over three of the double-pointed needles and cont in rounds of rib, working p2, [k2, p2] across the 14 cast-on sts, rib to end, ending at face opening.

Place a marker.

Next round [P2tog, k2] to end, slip marker. *51(57) sts.*

Next round [P1, k2] to end, slip marker.

Rep the last round twice more.

Next round [P1, skp] to end, slip marker. *34(38) sts.*

Next round [P1, k1] to end, slip marker.

Next round [K2tog] to end, slip marker. *17(19) sts.*

Next round K to end, slip marker.

Next round [K2tog] to last st, k1, slip marker. *9(10) sts.*

Next round K1(0), [k2tog] 4(5) times. *5 sts.*

Thread yarn through rem sts, pull to gather, and secure.

EARS MAKE 2

With size 8 (5mm) needles and B, cast on 3 sts.

1st row K1, p1, k1.

2nd row K1, p1, k1.

3rd row Work in seed st patt as set and inc at each end of row. *5 sts.*

4th row Seed st to end.

Rep the last 2 rows twice more. *9 sts.*

Work 10 rows in seed st.

Keeping seed st correct, dec 1 st at each end of next 3 rows. *3 sts.*

Next row K3tog and bind off.

Sew bound-off edge to side of head.

MOD DOG

Any dog will stand out as the leasher of the pack in this Mod-style sweater with its retro bullseye motif. This knit is the perfect attire for swinging around town on a souped-up scooter.

SIZES

Three sizes small (medium, large)—see coat measurements below and pages 8 and 9 to determine which size suits your dog

Measurements of knitted coat

Length measured along back 12¾(16½, 20¾)"/32(41, 51.5)cm

Width measured around chest 15¾(20, 24½)"/39(50, 61)cm

MATERIALS

Two 1¾oz (50g) balls of Debbie Bliss Rialto DK (100% merino wool, double-knitting-weight) in green (A) approx 115yd/105m and one 1¾oz (50g) ball in ecru (B), blue (C), red (D), and gold (E) approx 115yd/105m each

Pair each of sizes 3 and 6 (3.25mm and 4mm) knitting needles

Set of four size 5 (3.75mm) double-pointed knitting needles

GAUGE

22 sts and 30 rows to 4"/10cm square over St st using size 6 (4mm) needles.

ABBREVIATIONS

See page 13.

BACK

With size 3 (3.25mm) needles and A, cast on 44(56,68) sts.

Rib row [K1, p1] to end.

Rep the last row 7(9,13) times more.

Change to size 6 (4mm) needles.

Beg with a k row, work 34(40,66) rows in St st.

Next row (right side) K9(15,21)A, k across 26 sts of 1st chart row, k9(15,21)A.

Next row P9(15,21)A, p across 26 sts 2nd chart row, p9(15,21)A.

Working correct chart rows, cont in St st until all 36 chart rows have been worked.

Cont with A only, work even for 10(26:26) rows more, so ending with a p row.

SHAPE BACK

Next row K2, skp, k to last 4 sts, k2tog, k2.

Next row P to end.

Rep the last 2 rows 1(2,3) times more. *40(50,60) sts.*

Leave these sts on a holder.

FRONT

Omitting the chart, work as given for Back, until Front measures 3½(6,6)"/9(15,15)cm from cast-on edge, ending with a p row.

SHAPE FOR LEGHOLES

Bind off 10(12,12) sts at beg of next 2 rows. *24(32,44) sts.*

Work even for 16(24,24) rows more.

Cast on 10(12,12) sts at beg of next 2 rows. *44(56,68) sts.*

Work even until 12(14,18) rows fewer have been worked than on Back to lower back shaping.

SHAPE LOWER EDGE

Next row (right side) K13(16,19) sts, turn and work on these sts only for first side of shaping, leaving rem sts on a spare needle.

Dec one st at inside edge of next 12(15,18) rows.

Bind off rem st.

With right side facing, slip center 18(24,30) sts onto a holder, rejoin yarn to rem 13(16,19) sts on spare needle, k to end.

Dec one st at inside edge of next 12(15,18) rows.

Bind off rem st.

LOWER EDGING

Sew right side seam (from cast-on edges to beginning of lower back shaping), leaving leghole edge open.

With right side facing and size 6 (4mm) needles, pick up and k 11(14,17) sts down left side of front shaping, k across 18(24,30) sts at center front, pick up and k 11(14,17) sts up right side of front shaping, 4(6,8) sts up shaped edge of back, k across 40(50,60) sts at center back, pick up and k 4(6,8) sts down shaped edge of back. *88(114,140) sts.*

Rib row [K1, p1] to end.

Rep the last row 3(4,4) times more.

Bind off loosely in rib.

LEGHOLE EDGINGS

Sew left side seam, leaving leghole edge open.

With right side facing and 3.75mm (US 5) double-pointed needles, pick up and k 48(62,62) sts around leghole edge.

Arrange sts over three of the needles.

1st round [K1, p1] to end.

Rep the last round 3(4,4) times more.

Bind off loosely in rib.

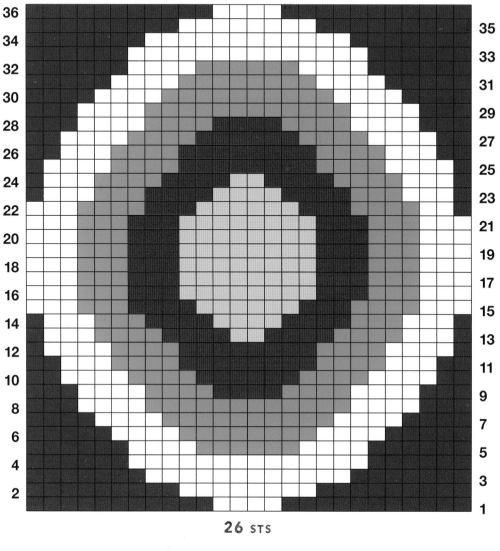

36
34
32
30
28
26
24
22
20
18
16
14
12
10
8
6
4
2

35
33
31
29
27
25
23
21
19
17
15
13
11
9
7
5
3
1

26 STS

KEY

■ A □ B ■ C ■ D ■ E

PIRATE POOCH

PIRATE POOCH

Avast, me hearties! Whether a Black Beard or a Red Beard, in the hunt for hidden treasure every Pirate Pooch must sport the traditional paw and crossbones motif, otherwise known as the The Jolly Rover.

SIZES

Two sizes small/medium (medium/large)—see coat measurements below and pages 8 and 9 to determine which size suits your dog

Measurements of knitted coat

Length measured along back 12¼(14¼)"/31(36)cm

Width measured around chest (excluding straps) 12½(15¼)"/32(39)cm

Note: Measurements given in the instructions are adjustable depending on your dog.

MATERIALS

2(3) x 1¾oz (50g) balls of Debbie Bliss Rialto DK (100% merino wool, double-knitting weight) black (A) approx 230(345)yd/210(315)m
and one 1¾oz (50g) ball in ecru (B) approx 115yd/105m

Pair each of sizes 5 and 6 (3.75mm and 4mm) knitting needles

Piece of black hook-and-loop fastener, 2"/5cm square

½yd/50cm of cotton fabric, for lining, and matching sewing thread

GAUGE

22 sts and 30 rows to 4"/10cm square over St st using size 6 (4mm) needles.

ABBREVIATIONS

wrap 1 bring yarn forward between needles, slip the next st, take the yarn back between needles, slip the wrapped st back onto left hand needle. When working back across a wrapped st in a subsequent row, work the st and the wrap together.

Also see page 13.

COAT

The coat and straps are worked in one piece.

With 3.75mm (US 5) needles and A, cast on 59(65) sts.

K 3 rows.

Change to size 6 (4mm) needles.

1st row K3, M1, k to last 3 sts, M1, k3.

2nd row K3, p to last 3 sts, k3.

Rep the 1st and 2nd rows 5(10) times more. *71(87) sts.*

Next row K to end.

Next row K3, p to last 3 sts, k3.

Rep the last 2 rows 7(9) times more.

Keeping sts at each side of the chart in A, work as follows:

Next row (right side) K23(31), k across 25 sts of 1st chart row, k23(31).

Next row K3, p20(28), p across 25 sts of 2nd chart row, p20(28), k3.

The last 2 rows set the position of the chart.

Working correct chart rows, cont as set until first 22 chart rows have been worked, so ending with a wrong-side row.

CHEST STRAPS

Next row Cast on 24 sts, k47(55), k25 sts of 23rd chart row, k23(31).

Next row Cast on 24, k27, p20(28), p25 sts of 24th chart row, p20(28), k27. *119(135) sts.*

Next row K47(55), k25 sts of 25th chart row, k47(55)A.

Next row K27, p20(28), p25 sts of 26th chart row, p20(28), k27.

Working correct chart rows, work even as set until all 39 chart rows have been worked.

Cont with A only.

Next row K27, p65(81), k27.

Next row K to end.

Next row Bind off 24 sts knitwise, k next 2 sts, p65(81), k3, bind off rem 24 sts knitwise. *71(87) sts.*

SHAPE NECK

With right side facing, rejoin yarn to first st.

1st and 2nd rows K23, wrap 1, turn, p to last 3 sts, k3.

3rd and 4th rows K21, wrap 1, turn, p to last 3 sts, k3.

5th and 6th rows K19, wrap 1, turn, p to last 3 sts, k3.

7th and 8th rows K17, wrap 1, turn, p to last 3 sts, k3.

9th and 10th rows K15, wrap 1, turn, p to last 3 sts, k3.

11th and 12th rows K13, wrap 1, turn, p to last 3 sts, k3.

13th and 14th rows K11, wrap 1, turn, p to last 3 sts, k3.

15th and 16th rows K9, wrap 1, turn, p to last 3 sts, k3.

17th and 18th rows K7, wrap 1, turn, p to last 3 sts, k3.

19th and 20th rows K5, wrap 1, turn, p to last 3 sts, k3.

21st row K to end, knitting wrap together with wrapped st.

22nd and 23rd rows K3, p20, wrap 1, turn, k to end.

24th and 25th rows K3, p18, wrap 1, turn, k to end.

26th and 27th rows K3, p16, wrap 1, turn, k to end.

28th and 29th rows K3, p14, wrap 1, turn, k to end.

30th and 31st rows K3, p12, wrap 1, turn, k to end.

32nd and 33rd rows K3, p10, wrap 1, turn, k to end.

34th and 35th rows K3, p8, wrap 1, turn, k to end.

36th and 37th rows K3, p6, wrap 1, turn, k to end.

38th and 39th rows K3, p4, wrap 1, turn, k to end.

40th and 41st rows K3, p2, wrap 1, turn, k to end.

42nd row K3, p to last 3 sts, purling wrap together with wrapped st, k3.

NECK STRAPS

1st row Cast on 18 sts, k to end.

2nd row Cast on 18 sts, k21, p65(81), k21. *107(123) sts.*

3rd row K to end.

4th row K21, p65(81), k21.

5th row K to end.

6th row K3, p to last 3 sts, k3.

7th–10th rows Rep 5th and 6th rows twice more.

11th row K7(11), [skp, k8] 4 times, skp, k9(17), k2tog, [k8, k2tog] 4 times, k7(11). *97(113) sts.*

12th–17th rows Rep 6th and 5th rows 3 times.

K 2 rows.

Bind off.

LINING

Lightly press the knitted coat on the wrong side, then lay it on the lining fabric and cut around the edge, adding ½"/1cm extra all around for the hem. Folding the hem onto the wrong side, slipstitch the lining to the coat.

TO FINISH

Cut the hook-and-loop fastener in half and sew one loop piece to the wrong side of the end of the neck strap and another to the wrong side of the end of the chest strap. Sew the loop pieces to the right sides of the neck and chest straps to match.

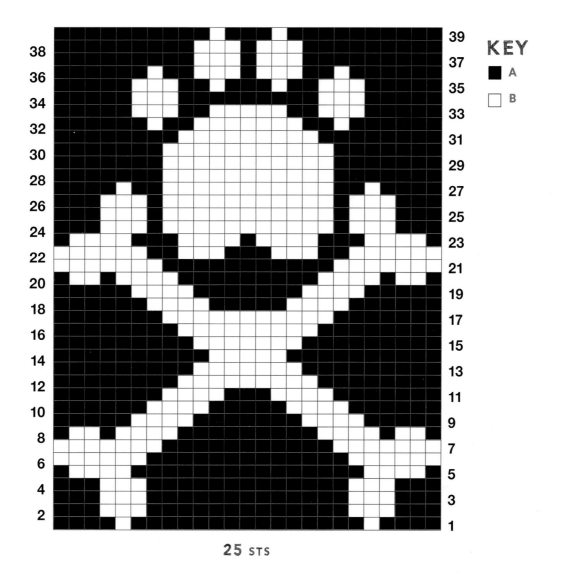

25 STS

CHART NOTES

When working from this chart, work all odd-numbered right-side rows from right to left in knit stitch and work all even-numbered wrong-side rows from left to right in purl stitch. Work the stitches in either yarn A or yarn B as appropriate. This color motif is worked using the intarsia method. Use separate strands or small balls of yarn for each color area and then twist them together where they meet to prevent a gap from forming.

LE CHIEN À LA MODE

Breton stripes and a jaunty beret are the epitome of canine chic. This delightfully Gallic combo will be coveted by all four-legged fashionistas who crave a wardrobe full of Chien-el and Pooch-ini.

SIZES

Two sizes small (medium)—see coat measurements below and pages 8 and 9 to determine which size suits your dog

Measurements of knitted coat

Length measured along back 13(16)in/33(41)cm

Width measured around chest 16(21¾)in/40(54.5)cm

MATERIALS

2(3) x 1¾oz (50g) balls each of Debbie Bliss Mia (50% cotton, 50% wool; double-knitting weight) in white (A) and marine blue (B), approx 218(327)yd/200(300)m each and small amount in ruby red (C)

Pair each of sizes 3 and 6 (3.25mm and 4mm) knitting needles

Set of four size 3 (3.25mm) double-pointed knitting needles

Length of black shirring elastic for beret

GAUGE

22 sts and 28 rows to 4"/10cm square over St st using size 6 (4mm) needles

ABBREVIATIONS

See page 13.

BACK OF COAT

With size 3 (3.25mm) needles and B, cast on *44(60) sts.*

K 5 rows.

Change to size 6 (4mm) needles.

Beg with a k row, work in St st until Back measures 3½(4½)"/9(11)cm from cast-on edge, ending with a p row.**

Cont in St st and stripes of 2 rows B and 6 rows A, until Back measures 10¼(13½)"/26(34)cm from cast-on edge, ending with a 6-row A stripe.

Cont in stripe sequence and work as follows:

Next row (right side) K to end.

Next row K3, p to last 3 sts, k3.

Rep the last 2 rows 7 times more, so ending with a 6-row A stripe.

Change to size 3 (3.25mm) needles and B.

K 3 rows.

Bind off.

FRONT OF COAT

Work as given for Back to **.

Beg with a k row, work 2 rows B and 6 rows A in St st.

SHAPE FOR LEGHOLES

Cont in stripe sequence as given for Back, working as follows:

Bind off 10(12) sts at beg of next 2 rows. *24(36) sts.*

Work 16 rows more.

Cast on 10(12) sts at beg of next 2 rows. *44(60) sts.*

Cont in St st and stripe sequence until Front measures 10¼(13½)"/26(34)cm from cast-on edge, ending with a 6-row A stripe.

Change to size 3 (3.25mm) needles and B.

K 3 rows.

Bind off.

LEGHOLE EDGINGS

Sew side seams, leaving leghole edges open.

With right side facing, size 3 (3.25mm) double-pointed needles and A, pick up and k 48(52) sts around leghole edge.

Arrange sts over three of the needles.

Rib round [K1, p1] to end.

Rib 4 rounds more.

Bind off loosely in rib.

BERET

With size 3 (3.25mm) needles and B, cast on 64 sts.

K 5 rows.

Change to size 6 (4mm) needles.

Inc row K5, [M1, k1, M1, k8] 6 times, M1, k1, M1, k4. *78 sts.*

K 3 rows.

Inc row K6, [M1, k1, M1, k10] 6 times, M1, k1, M1, k5. *92 sts.*

K 3 rows.

Inc row K7, [M1, k1, M1, k12] 6 times, M1, k1, M1, k6. *106 sts*

K 8 rows.

Dec row K6, [skp, k1, k2tog, k10] 6 times, skp, k1, k2tog, k5. *92 sts.*

K 4 rows.

Dec row K5, [skp, k1, k2tog, k8] 6 times, skp, k1, k2tog, k4. *78 sts.*

K 4 rows.

Dec row K4, [skp, k1, k2tog, k6] 6 times, skp, k1, k2tog, k3. *64 sts.*

K 4 rows.

Dec row K3, [skp, k1, k2tog, k4] 6 times, skp, k1, k2tog, k2. *50 sts.*

K 4 rows.

Dec row K2, [skp, k1, k2tog, k2] 6 times, skp, k1, k2tog, k1. *36 sts.*

K 4 rows.

Dec row K1, [skp, k1, k2tog] 6 times, skp, k1, k2tog. *22 sts.*

K 1 row.

Dec row [K2tog] to end. *11 sts.*

Cut off yarn, thread end through rem sts, pull to gather, and secure.

TO FINISH BERET

Sew beretseam.

With C, make a pompom 1½"/4cm in diameter and sew securely to the top of the beret.

Attach a length of shirring elastic to the beret to keep it in place on your dog's head.

PAW-
KERCHIEFS

PAW SCARF

The finishing sartorial touch for any dapper dog is a jaunty paw-kerchief tied around the neck. Take your pick of this paw-print scarf or the Scottie version on page 58.

SIZE

One size approximately 17in/43cm wide and 8¼"/21cm deep

MATERIALS

One 1¾oz (50g) ball of Debbie Bliss Baby Cashmerino (55% wool, 33% microfiber, 12% cashmere; fine-weight) in royal blue (A) and small amount in white (B) approx 136yd/125m

Pair of size 3 (3.25mm) knitting needles

Small piece of black hook-and-loop fastener

GAUGE

25 sts and 34 rows to 4"/10cm square over St st using size 3 (3.25mm) needles.

ABBREVIATIONS

See page 13.

CHART NOTES

When working from this chart, work all odd-numbered right-side rows from right to left in knit stitch and work all even-numbered wrong-side rows from left to right in purl stitch. Work the stitches in either yarn A or yarn B as appropriate. This color motif is worked using the intarsia method. Use separate strands or small balls of yarn for each color area and then twist them together where they meet to prevent a gap from forming.

TO MAKE

With size 3 (3.25mm) needles and A, cast on 107 sts.

1st row (right side) K to end.

2nd row P to end.

3rd row (right side) K2, skp, k to last 4 sts, k2tog, k2.

4th row P2, p2tog, p to last 4 sts, p2tog tbl, p2.

5th row K2, skp, k to last 4 sts, k2tog, k2.

6th row P to end.

Rep 3rd–6th rows 8 times more, then the 3rd and 4th rows again. *49 sts.*

Next row (as 5th row) K2, skp, k13, k across 15 sts of 1st row of paw chart, k13, k2tog, k2.

Next row (as 6th row) P16, p across 15 sts of 2nd row of chart, p16.

The last 2 rows **set** the position of the chart.

Working the correct chart rows, cont to rep the 3rd–6th rows, so decreasing at each edge until the 18th chart row has been worked. *23 sts.*

Cont with A only and beg with a 3rd row, cont to dec as before until 3 sts remain, so ending with a 3rd row.

Bind off.

TO FINISH

Sew hook-and-loop fastener to the scarf, the hook piece to the wrong side of one end and the loop piece to the right side of other end.

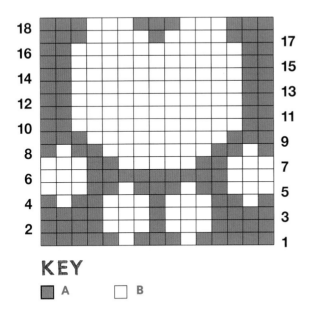

KEY

■ A   □ B

SCOTTIE SCARF

Another jaunty paw-kerchief for the discerning pooch. For a customized scarf, devise your own design by drawing your dog's silhouette on knitter's graph paper.

SIZE

One size approximately 17"/43cm wide and 8¼"/21cm deep

MATERIALS

One 1¾oz (50g) ball of Debbie Bliss Baby Cashmerino (55% wool, 33% microfiber, 12% cashmere; fine-weight) in pink (A) approx 136yd/125m
and small amount in white (B), red (C), and black (D)
Pair of size 3 (3.25mm) knitting needles
Small piece of black hook-and-loop fastener

GAUGE

25 sts and 34 rows to 4"/10cm square over St st using size 3 (3.25mm) needles.

ABBREVIATIONS

See page 13.

CHART NOTES

When working from this chart, work all odd-numbered right-side rows from right to left in knit stitch and work all even-numbered wrong-side rows from left to right in purl stitch. Work the stitches in either yarn A or yarn B as appropriate. This color motif is worked using the intarsia method. Use separate strands or small balls of yarn for each color area and then twist them together where they meet to prevent a gap from forming. Embroider yarn C using duplicate stitch on completion.

TO MAKE

With size 3 (3.25mm) needles and A, cast on 107 sts.

1st row (right side) K to end.

2nd row P to end.

3rd row (right side) K2, skp, k to last 4 sts, k2tog, k2.

4th row P2, p2tog, p to last 4 sts, p2tog tbl, p2.

5th row K2, skp, k to last 4 sts, k2tog, k2.

6th row P to end.

Rep 3rd–6th rows 6 times more. *65 sts.*

Next row (as 3rd row) K2, skp, k21, k across 15 sts of 1st row of Scottie chart, k21, k2tog, k2.

Next row (as 4th row) P2, p2tog, p20, p across 15 sts of 2nd row of chart, p20, p2tog tbl, p2.

The last 2 rows set the position of the chart.

Working the correct chart rows, cont to rep the 3rd–6th rows (next row will be a 5th row), decreasing at each edge until the 15th chart row has been worked. *41 sts.*

Cont with A only and beg with a 6th row, cont to dec as before until 3 sts remain, so ending with a 3rd row.

Bind off.

TO FINISH

Duplicate stitch the Scottie's collar in C and work a stitch in D to mark the dog's eye.

Sew hook-and-loop fastener to the scarf, the hook piece to the wrong side of one end and the loop piece to the right side of other end.

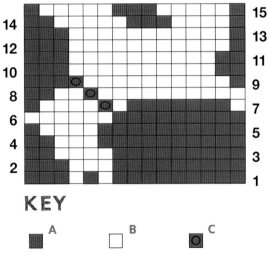

KEY

A ▪   B ▫   C ◉

Duplicate stitch C on completion of knitting

COWBOY
BANDANA

COWBOY BANDANA

Howdy! Whether wrangling cattle on the open range, riding the bucking bronco at the local cowboy meetup, or dancing the dosey doe at a hoedown, all Rodeo Rovers will stay smart with this fringed bandana.

SIZE

One size approximately 19"/48cm wide and 8"/20cm deep

MATERIALS

One 1¾oz (50g) ball of Debbie Bliss Baby Cashmerino (55% wool,
33% microfiber, 12% cashmere; fine-weight) in
each of navy (A), amber (B), and red (C) 136yd/125m each

Pair of size 3 (3.25mm) knitting needles

Two black snaps

GAUGE

25 sts and 34 rows to 4"/10cm square over St st using size 3 (3.25mm) needles.

ABBREVIATIONS

See page 13.

TO MAKE

With size 3 (3.25mm) needles and A, cast on 3 sts.

Foundation row (wrong side) [P1, yo] twice, p1. *5 sts.*

1st row K to end.

2nd row P1, yo, p to last st, yo, p1.

3rd row K1, yo, k to last st, yo, k1.

4th row P1, yo, p to last st, yo, p1.

The last 4 rows form the basic pattern and are repeated.

Work 12 rows more in patt. *29 sts.*

17th row K7, k across 15 sts of 1st row of chart, k7.

18th row P1, yo, p6, p across 2nd row of chart, p6, yo, p1.

19th row K1, yo, k7, k across 3rd row of chart, k7, yo, k1.

20th row P1, yo, p8, p across 4th row of chart, p8, yo, p1. *35 sts.*

Taking inc sts into St st and working correct chart rows, cont to rep the 4 patt rows, keeping the chart in position as set until all 20 chart rows have been completed. *59 sts.*

Beg with 1st row, cont in basic patt in A only, repeating the 4 patt rows 8 times more. *107 sts.*

SHAPE FIRST SIDE OF NECK

69th row K46, turn and leave rem sts on the needle.

70th row Sl 1, p to last st, yo, p1.

71st row K1, yo, k34, turn.

72nd row Sl 1, p to last st, yo, p1.

73rd row K25, turn.

74th row Sl 1, p to last st, yo, p1.

75th row K1, yo, k13, turn.

76th row Sl 1, p to last st, yo, p1.

77th row K4, turn.

78th row Sl 1, p2, yo, p1. *5 sts.*

79th row K across all sts.

SHAPE SECOND SIDE OF NECK

70th row P1, yo, p45, turn.

71st row Sl 1, k to last st, yo, k1.

72nd row P1, yo, p35, turn.

73rd row Sl 1, k to end.

74th row P1, yo, p24, turn.

75th row Sl 1, k to last st, yo, k1.

76th row P1, yo, p14, turn.

77th row Sl 1, k to end.

78th row P1, yo, p3. *5 sts.*

79th row Sl 1, k to end.

Bind off all 121 sts knitwise on wrong side.

TO FINISH

Cut two 2¼"/6cm lengths of C for each of the eyelets created on the increase rows. Fold the two lengths in half, then with the wrong side of the neckerchief facing and starting at the point, insert the crochet hook through each eyelet in turn and pull the folded end of the yarn lengths through. Take the ends of the lengths through the loop and pull tightly. When all the fringe has been added to the eyelets, trim the ends to neaten.

Overlap the neck edge of the neckerchief and sew snaps to the points to fasten it in place around your dog's neck.

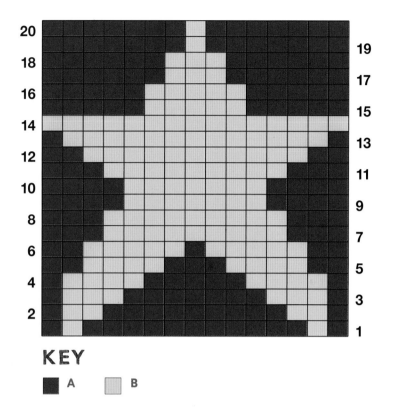

KEY

■ A   ▢ B

CHART NOTES

When working from this chart, work all odd-numbered right-side rows from right to left in knit stitch and work all even-numbered wrong-side rows from left to right in purl stitch. Work the stitches in either yarn A or yarn B as appropriate. This color motif is worked using the intarsia method. Use separate strands or small balls of yarn for each color area and then twist them together where they meet to prevent a gap from forming.

COW
BOW-
WOW

COW BOW-WOW

Forget Jerseys and Guernseys, the knitwear to be wearing at the moment is Freisian. This sweater coat with its black and white markings will not necessarily make your dog stand out from the crowd, but rather appear part of the herd.

SIZES

Two sizes small/medium (medium/large)—see coat measurements below and pages 8 and 9 to determine which size suits your dog

Measurements of knitted coat

Length measured along back 16½(19½)"/42(50)cm

Width measured around chest 21¼(24¾)"/54(63)cm

MATERIALS

3(4) x 1¾oz (50g) balls of Debbie Bliss Blue Faced Leicester Aran (100% wool, aran-weight) in ecru (A) approx 246(328)yd/225(300)m
and one 1¾oz (50g) ball in black (B) approx 82 yd/75m

Pair each of sizes 7 and 8 (4.5mm and 5mm) knitting needles

Set of four size 7 (4.5mm) double-pointed knitting needles

GAUGE

18 sts and 24 rows to 4"/10cm over St st using size 8 (5mm) needles.

NOTE

⨝ This coat is worked from the neck down.

BACK

With size 7 (4.5mm) needles and A, cast on 46(54) sts.

1st rib row K2, [p2, k2] to end.

2nd rib row P2, [k2, p2] to end.

Rep these 2 rows 4 times more and inc 4 sts evenly across last row. *50(58) sts.*

Change to size 8 (5mm) needles and beg with a k row, work 2(16) rows in St st.

Next row (right side) K3(7)A, k across 44 sts of 1st row of chart, k3(7)A.

Next row P3(7)A, p across 44 sts of 2nd row of chart, p3(7)A.

The last 2 rows **set** the position of the chart.

Working correct chart rows, cont until all 76 chart rows have been worked.

Beg with a k row, cont in St st in A only until Back measures 15(18)"/38(46)cm from cast-on edge, ending with a p row.

SHAPE LOWER BACK

Next row K2, skp, k to last 4 sts, k2tog, k2.

Next row P to end.

Rep the last 2 rows once more. *46(54) sts.*

Leave these sts on a holder.

FRONT

Omitting the chart, work as given for Back until Front measures 6(6½)"/15(17)cm from cast-on edge, ending with a p row.

SHAPE FOR LEGHOLES

Bind off 8(10) sts at beg of next 2 rows. *34(38) sts.*

Work 14(16) rows more.

Cast on 8(10) sts at beg of next 2 rows. *50(58) sts.*

Work even until 12 rows fewer have been worked than on Back to lower back shaping.

SHAPE LOWER EDGE

Next row (right side) K14, turn and work on these sts only for first side of shaping, leaving rem sts on a spare needle.

Dec one st at inside edge on next 11 rows. *3 sts.*

Next row K3tog and bind off.

With right side facing, slip center 22(30) sts onto a holder, rejoin yarn, k to end.

Dec one st at inside edge on next 11 rows. *3 sts.*

Next row K3tog and bind off.

LOWER EDGING

Sew right side seam (from cast-on edges to beginning of lower back shaping), leaving leghole edge open.

With right side facing, size 7 (4.5mm) needles, and A, pick up and k 11 sts down left front shaping, k across 22(30) sts at center front, pick up and k 11 sts up right front shaping, 4 sts up right back shaping, k across 46(54) sts at lower back, then pick up and k 4 sts down left back shaping. *98(114) sts.*

1st rib row P2, [k2, p2] to end.

2nd rib row K2, [p2, k2] to end.

Rep the last 2 rows twice more.

Bind off in rib.

LEGHOLE EDGINGS

Sew left side seam, leaving leghole edge open.

With right side facing, size 7 (4.5mm) double-pointed needles and A, pick up and k 38(44) sts around leg opening.

Arrange sts over three of the needles.

Rib round [K1, p1] to end.

Rib 3 rounds more.

Bind off in rib.

KEY

A   B

44 STS

CHART NOTES

When working from this chart, work all odd-numbered right-side rows from right to left in knit stitch and work all even-numbered wrong-side rows from left to right in purl stitch. Work the stitches in either yarn A or yarn B as appropriate. This color motif is worked using the intarsia method. Use separate strands or small balls of yarn for each color area and then twist them together where they meet to prevent a gap from forming.

MARDI GRAS MUTT

MARDI GRAS MUTT

Every day is a fun-filled fiesta when wearing colorful rainbow stripes. For those dogs who are more carnival than carnivore, this joyful sweater will be the pride of their canine closet.

SIZES

Three sizes small (medium, large)—see coat measurements below and pages 8 and 9 to determine which size suits your dog

Measurements of knitted coat

Length measured along back 12¾(16¼,19¾)"/32(41,50)cm
Width measured around chest 15¼(19¾,24)"/38(50,61)cm

MATERIALS

One 1¾oz (50g) ball of Debbie Bliss Rialto DK (100% merino wool, double-knitting-weight) in each of six colors—red (A), orange (B), yellow (C), green (D), blue (E), and purple (F) approx 115yd/105m each

Pair each of sizes 3 and 6 (3.25mm and 4mm) knitting needles

Set of four size 5 (3.75mm) double-pointed knitting needles

GAUGE

22 sts and 30 rows to 4"/10cm square over St st using size 6 (4mm) needles.

ABBREVIATIONS

See page 13.

BACK

With size 3 (3.25mm) needles and A, cast on 44(56,68) sts.

Rib row [K1, p1] to end.

Rep the last row 7(9,13) times more.

Change to size 6 (4mm) needles.

Beg with a k row, work in St st and stripes of 6 rows B, 6 rows C, 6 rows D, 6 rows E, 6 rows F, 6 rows A, until 80(102,122) rows in St st have been worked.

SHAPE LOWER BACK

Keeping stripe sequence correct, work as follows:

Next row (right side) K2, skp, k to last 4 sts, k2tog, k2.

Next row P to end.

Rep the last 2 rows 1(2,3) times more.

Leave these 40(50,60) sts on a holder.

FRONT

Work as given for Back until 20(36,36) rows in St st have been completed.

SHAPE FOR LEGHOLES

Keeping stripe sequence correct, work as follows:

Bind off 10(12,12) sts at beg of next 2 rows. *24(32,44) sts.*

Work 16(24,24) rows more.

Cast on 10(12,12) sts at beg of next 2 rows. *44(56,68) sts.*

Work even until 12(16,18) rows fewer have been worked than on Back to lower back shaping, so ending with a p row.

SHAPE LOWER EDGE

Next row (right side) K13(16,19), turn and work on these sts only for first side of shaping,

leaving rem sts on a spare needle.

Dec one st at inside edge on next 12(15,18) rows.

Bind off rem st.

With right side facing, slip center 18(24,30) sts onto a holder, rejoin yarn to rem 13(16,19) sts, k to end.

Dec one st at inside edge on next 12(15,18) rows.

Bind off rem st.

LOWER EDGING

Sew right side seam (from cast-on edges to beginning of lower back shaping), leaving leghole edge open.

With right side facing, size 6 (4mm) needles and B, pick up and k 11(14,17) sts down left front edge, k across 18(24,30) sts at center front, pick up and k 11(14,17) sts up right front edge, 4(6,8) sts up shaped edge of back, k across 40(50,60) sts at lower back, pick up and k 4(6,8) sts down shaped edge of back. *88(114,140) sts.*

Rib row [K1, p1] to end.

Rep the last row 3(4,4) times more

Bind off loosely in rib.

LEGHOLE EDGINGS

Sew left side seam, leaving leghole edge open.

With right side facing, 3.75mm (US 5) double-pointed needles, and B, pick up and k 48(62,62) sts around leg opening.

Arrange sts over three of the needles.

1st round [K1, p1] to end.

Rib 3(4,4) rounds more.

Bind off loosely in rib.

MAN'S BEE FRIEND

Don't get a bee in your bonnet, get a bee on your bonnet! Dressed in this stripey bumblebee costume, topped off with a hat and antennae, your dog will be perfectly dressed for an afternoon of buzzing around.

SIZES

Two sizes small (medium)—see coat measurements below and pages 8 and 9 to determine which size suits your dog

Measurements of knitted coat

Length measured along back 14¼(18)"/36(46)cm

Width measured around chest 14(19)"/35.5(48)cm

MATERIALS

One 1¾oz (50g) ball of Debbie Bliss Cashmerino Aran (55% wool, 33% microfiber, 12% cashmere; aran-weight) in black (A) and one 1¾oz (50g) ball in yellow (B) approx 98yd/90m each

Pair of size 8 (5mm) knitting needles

Set of four size 7 (4.5mm) double-pointed knitting needles

Optional black pipe cleaners to shape the antennae

GAUGE

18 sts and 24 rows to 4"/10cm square over St st using size 8 (5mm) needles.

ABBREVIATIONS

See page 13.

COAT WORKED ALL IN ONE

With size 8 (5mm) needles and A, cast on 39(61) sts.

1st row K3, [p1, k1] to last 2 sts, k2.

2nd row K2, [p1, k1] to last 3 sts, p1, k2.

These 2 rows form rib with garter st at each side.

Rep the last 2 rows 3 times more.

Change to B.

Next row K to end.

Next row K2, p to last 2 sts, k2.

The last 2 rows form St st and continue the garter st at each side.

Rep the last 2 rows once more.

Change to A.

Rep the last 4 rows once.

Rep this 8-row stripe sequence 2(3) times more, then work 4 rows in B.

Next row (right side) With A, cast on 25 sts, work k1, [p1, k1] 12 times across these 25 cast-on sts, k rem 39(61) sts. *64(86) sts.*

Next row K2, p35(57), k2, p1, [k1, p1] to end.

Next row Rib 25, k39(61).

Next row K2, p35(57), k2, p1, [k1, p1] to end.

Next row With A, rib 25, with B, k39(61).

Next row With B, k2, p35(57), k2, with A, rib to end.

Rep the last 2 rows once more.

With right side facing, slip first 25 sts onto a holder, work 32(48) rows in stripe sequence as before on rem 39(61) sts, so ending with 4 rows in B.

Slip these sts onto a spare needle.

UNDERSIDE

With RS facing, rejoin A to 25 sts on holder, k to end.

Cont in A only.

1ST SIZE ONLY

Next row K2, p to last 2 sts, k2.

** 1st dec row (right side) K2, skp, k to last 4 sts, k2tog, k2.

Next row K2, p to last 2 sts, k2.

Next row K to end.

Rep the last 2 rows once more.

2nd dec row (wrong side) K2, p2tog, p to last 4 sts, p2tog tbl, k2.

Next row K to end.

Next row K2, p to last 2 sts, k2.

Rep the last 2 rows once more.

Rep the last 10 rows from ** twice more, so ending with a wrong-side row. *13 sts.*

2ND SIZE ONLY

*** Next row (wrong side) K2, p to last 2 sts, k2.

1st dec row (right side) K2, skp, k to last 4 sts, k2tog, k2.

Next row K2, p to last 2 sts, k2.

Next row K to end.

Rep the last 2 rows twice more.

Now rep the last 8 rows from *** 4 times more, then the first 5 of these 8 rows again, so ending with a wrong-side row. *13 sts.*

BOTH SIZES

Next row (right side) K12, k last st tog with 1st st on spare needle, k to end. *51(73) sts.*

Next row (wrong side) P1, [k1, p1] to end.

Next row K1, [p1, k1] to end.

Rep the last 2 rows 4 times more.

Bind off loosely in rib.

HAT

With size 7 (4.5mm) double-pointed needles and A, cast on 68(72) sts.

Being careful not to twist the cast-on edge, arrange sts over three of the needles to work in rounds.

Rib round [K2, p2] to end.

Rep this round 12(16) times more.

SHAPE FOR FACE

Next round K2, [p2, k2] twice, bind off next 14(18) sts in rib, rib to end. *54 sts.*

Working backward and forward in rows on two needles in rib as set, cont for a further 2¼"/6cm, ending with a wrong-side row.

Next row Cast on 14(18) sts, work p2, [k2, p2] across these cast-on sts, then rib across remaining 54 sts and place a marker. *68(72) sts.*

Arrange sts over three of the double-pointed needles to work in rounds.

Dec round [P2tog, k2] to end, slip marker. *51(54) sts.*

Next round [P1, k2] to end, slip marker.

Rep last round twice more.

Next round [P1, skp] to end, slip marker. *34(36) sts.*

Next round [P1, k1] to end, slip marker.

Next round [K2tog] to end, slip marker. *17(18) sts.*

Next round K to end, slip marker.

Next round [K2tog] to last 1(0) st, k1(0), slip marker. *9 sts.*

Next round [K2tog] 4 times, k1. *5 sts.*

Thread yarn through remaining 5 sts on needle, pull to gather, and secure.

ANTENNAE MAKE 2

With size 7 (4.5mm) double-pointed needles, cast on 5 sts.

Use two double-pointed needles to work each antenna as follows:

K 1 row.

Next row Slip all 5 sts to the other end of needle, pull the yarn tightly from the last st and k the 5 sts.

Rep the last row, so forming a tube, until antenna measures approximately 3½in/9cm from cast-on edge.

Thread the yarn through the sts, pull to gather, and secure.

If you want to shape the antennae, pass a pipe cleaner through the center, then sew the antennae to the top of the hat.

GIVE-A-DOG-A-BONE COAT

GIVE-A-DOG-A-BONE COAT

While dogs love love nothing more than a juicy bone, sometimes bones don't love dogs and can cause serious injuries when eaten. So the safest way for a dog to enjoy a meaty bone is to wear a suede motif on a jaunty tweed jacket.

SIZES

Two sizes small/medium (medium/large)—see coat measurements below and pages 8 and 9 to determine which size suits your dog

Measurements of knitted coat

Length measured along back 13(15¼)"/33(39)cm

Width measured around chest (excluding straps) 11¾(14¼)"/30(36)cm

MATERIALS

Three 1¾oz (50g) balls of Debbie Bliss Luxury Tweed Aran (90% wool, 10% angora; aran-weight) in bronze approx 288yd/264m

Pair of size 8 (5mm) knitting needles

Size 7 (4.5mm) crochet hook

1yd/1m of cotton fabric, for lining, and matching sewing thread

Piece of black hook-and-loop fastener, 2"/5cm by 4"/10cm

Piece of brown suede, 8"/20cm by 3¼in/8cm, for bone motif

Two buttons

GAUGE

17 sts and 30 rows to 4"/10cm square over seed stitch using size 8 (5mm) needles.

ABBREVIATIONS

See page 13.

COAT

With size 8 (5mm) needles, cast on 35(45) sts.

Seed st row (wrong side) K1, [p1, k1] to end.

The last row forms seed st and is worked throughout.

Taking inc sts into seed st, inc 1 st each end of next row and 7 foll right-side rows. *51(61) sts.*

Work even until piece measures 10½(13¼)"/ 27(34)cm from cast-on edge, ending with a wrong-side row.

SHAPE SIDES

Inc and take into seed st, 1 st at each end of next row and 3 foll 4th rows. *59(69) sts.*

Work 3 rows.

SHAPE NECK

Next row (right side) Inc 1 st, patt until there are 22 sts on the right-hand needle, turn and work on these sts only, leaving rem sts on a spare needle.

Next row Dec 1 st, patt to end.

Next row Patt to last 2 sts, patt 2 tog.

Next row Dec 1 st, patt to end.

Next row Inc 1 st, patt to last 2 sts, patt 2 tog.

Rep the last 4 rows twice more. *13 sts.*

Patt 1 row.

Next row Patt to last 2 sts, patt 2 tog.

Rep the last 2 rows twice more. *10 sts.*

Work even for 2(8) rows (neck strap length can be adjusted here).

Next row Dec 1 st at each end of row. *8 sts.*

Bind off in patt.

With right side facing, rejoin yarn to sts on spare needle, bind off 17(27) center sts, patt to end and inc 1 st. *22 sts.*

Work to match first side of neck, reversing shapings.

CHEST STRAPS MAKE 2

With size 8 (5mm) needles, cast on 15 sts and work in seed st for 3½(6)"/9(15)cm or until strap, when attached to the coat will fit around your dog and overlap the corresponding strap on the other side.

Dec one st each end of foll 3 rows.

Bind off rem 9 sts.

Attach to each side of coat where appropriate for your dog.

EDGING

With right side facing and size 7 (4.5mm) crochet hook, work a row of single crochet all around the edge of the coat.

LINING

Lay the jacket on the lining fabric and cut around the edge, adding ½"/1cm extra all around for the hem.

Turn the hem onto the wrong side and slipstitch the lining to the coat.

Cut the hook-and-loop fastener in half and sew one loop piece to the right side of one neck strap end and one chest strap end, then one hook piece to the wrong side of the other end of the neck and chest straps to match.

Cut a bone shape, approximately 7½"/19cm long, from suede and stitch each end of the suede bone to the coat, sew on a button at each end.

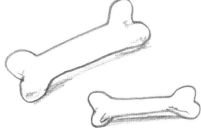

CLAN CANINE

ARGYLE COAT WITH SMALL SCOTTIES

Commemorate your dog's noble heritage with these traditional Argyle patterned coats. Choose between these multiple dog motifs or the single large terrier shape on page 91. Either way, every dog looks good in diamonds.

SIZES

Two sizes small/medium (medium/large)—see coat measurements below and pages 8 and 9 to determine which size suits your dog

Measurements of knitted coat

Length measured along back 13¾(14½)"/35(37)cm

Width measured around chest (excluding straps) 12(14)"/30(35.5)cm

Note: Measurements given in the instructions are adjustable depending on your dog.

MATERIALS

Two 1¾oz (50g) balls of Debbie Bliss Baby Cashmerino (55% wool, 33% microfiber, 12% cashmere; fine-weight) in blue (A) approx 272yd/250m and one 1¾oz (50g) ball in each ecru (B), ruby red (C), and black (D) approx 136yd/125m each

Pair of size 3 (3.25mm) knitting needles

Size 3 (3.25mm) circular knitting needle, 31½"/80cm long

Piece of black hook-and-loop fastener, 2"/5cm square, and matching sewing thread

GAUGE

25 sts and 34 rows to 4"/10cm square over main patt using size 3 (3.25mm) needles.

ABBREVIATIONS

Also see page 13.

COAT

With size 3 (3.25mm) needles and A, cast on 55(61) sts.

Seed st row (right side) K1, [p1, k1] to end.

This row forms the seed st and is repeated.

Work 5 rows more in seed st.

Next row (right side) Seed st 6, M1, k to last 6 sts, M1, seed st 6.

Next row Seed st 6, p to last 6 sts, seed st 6.

Rep the last 2 rows 5(9) times more. *67(81) sts.*

1st row Seed st 6, M1, k0(7), k across 55 sts of 1st chart row, k0(7), M1, seed st 6.

2nd row Seed st 6, p1(8), p across 55 sts of 2nd chart row, p1(8), seed st 6.

3rd row Seed st 6, M1, k1(8), k across 55 sts of 3rd chart row, k1(8), M1, seed st 6.

4th row Seed st 6, p2(9), p across 55 sts of 4th chart row, p2(9), seed st 6.

5th row Seed st 6, M1, k2(9), k across 55 sts of 5th chart row, k2(9), M1, seed st 6.

6th row Seed st 6, p3(10), p across 55 sts of 6th chart row, p3(10), seed st 6.

7th row Seed st 6, M1, k3(10), k across 55 sts of 7th chart row, k3(10), M1, seed st 6.

8th row Seed st 6, p4(11), p across 55 sts of 8th chart row, p4(11), seed st 6. *75(89) sts.*

Now work even, working 6 edge sts in seed st and central St st in patt from chart as set.

Work to end of 64th chart row, then work 15th–50th chart rows again.

Cont in A only, work 0(6) rows.

SHAPE NECK

Next row (right side) Seed st 6, k21, bind off center 21(35) sts, patt to end and cont on these 27 sts only, leaving rem 27 sts on a holder.

Next row Seed st 6, p to last 2 sts, p2tog.

Next row Bind off 2 sts, patt to end.

Rep these 2 rows 6 times more. *6 sts.*

Leave these 6 sts on a holder.

With wrong side facing, rejoin yarn to 27 sts on holder.

Next row Bind off 2 sts, patt to end.

Next row Patt to last 2 sts, k2tog.

Rep these 2 rows 6 times more. *6 sts.*

Next row Patt to end.

COLLAR

Pick-up row (right side) With size 3 (3.25mm) circular needle, seed st 6, pick up and k 63(77) sts evenly along neck edge, seed st 6 sts from holder, cast on 26 sts. *101(115) sts.*

With size 3 (3.25mm) needles and a spare length of A, cast on 26 sts and set aside.

With wrong side facing, return to 101(115) sts on circular needle, seed st to end, then seed st across 26 sts on needle. *127(141) sts.*

Work 11 rows in seed st.

Dec row Seed st 6, [p3tog, seed st 11] 8(9) times, p3tog, seed st 6. *109(121) sts.*

Work 11 rows in seed st.

Bind off in seed st.

CHEST STRAPS MAKE 2

With size 3 (3.25mm) needles and D, cast on 31 sts.

Work in seed st as for coat until strap measures 2¼"/6cm.

Bind off in seed st.

TO FINISH

Lay the coat on your dog to determine where to position the straps, then sew in place.

Cut the piece of hook-and-loop fastener in

half. Sew one hook piece to the wrong side of one end of the collar and one loop piece to the right side of the other end of the collar. Sew one hook piece to the wrong side of one strap and one loop piece to the right side of the other strap. Using duplicate stitch, embroider the diagonal lines and dog collars on the chart.

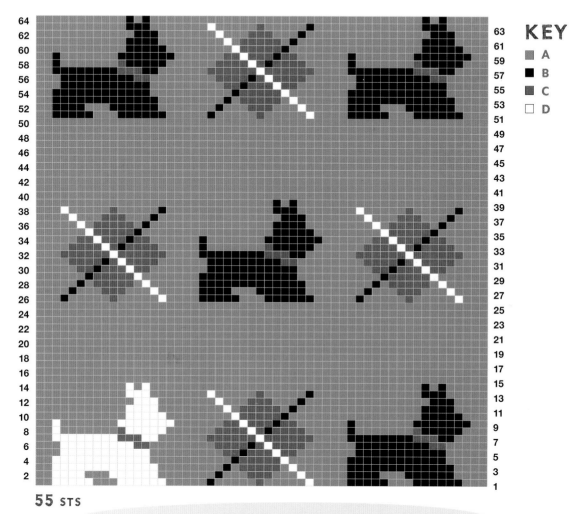

55 STS

KEY

- ■ A
- ■ B
- ■ C
- □ D

CHART NOTES

When working from this chart, work all odd-numbered right-side rows from right to left in knit stitch and work all even-numbered wrong-side rows from left to right in purl stitch. Work the stitches in either yarn A, B, C, or D as appropriate. This color motif is worked using the intarsia method. Use separate strands or small balls of yarn for each color area and then twist them together where they meet to prevent a gap from forming. Using duplicate stitch, embroider the diagonal lines and dog collars on completion.

ARGYLE COAT WITH LARGE SCOTTIE

If your dog isn't the type to show off with as many diamonds as those on the Argyle Coat on page 88, then keep his or her clan coat modest with a single large Scottie motif—it has the added advantage of being quicker to knit.

SIZES

Two sizes small/medium (medium/large)—see coat measurements below and pages 8 and 9 to determine which size suits your dog

Measurements of knitted coat

Length measured along back 13¾(14½)"/35(37)cm

Width measured around chest (excluding straps) 12(14)"/30(35.5)cm

MATERIALS

Two 1¾oz (50g) balls of Debbie Bliss Baby Cashmerino (55% wool, 33% microfiber, 12% cashmere; fine-weight) in ruby red (A) approx 272yd/250m, one 1¾oz (50g) ball in blue (B) approx 136yd/125m, and small amounts in ecru (C) and black (D)

Pair of size 3 (3.25mm) knitting needles

Size 3 (3.25mm) circular knitting needle, 31½"/80cm long

Piece of black hook-and-loop fastener, 2"/5cm square, and matching sewing thread

GAUGE

25 sts and 34 rows to 4"/10cm square over main patt using size 3 (3.25mm) needles.

ABBREVIATIONS

See page 13.

COAT

With size 3 (3.25mm) needles and A, cast on 59(65) sts.

Seed st row (right side) K1, [p1, k1] to end.

This row forms the seed st and is repeated.

Work 5 rows more in seed st.

Next row (right side) Seed st 6, M1, k to last 6 sts, M1, seed st 6.

Next row Seed st 6, p to last 6 sts, k1.

Rep the last 2 rows 7(11) times more. *75(89) sts.*

1st row (right side) Seed st 6A, k11(18)A, k across 41 sts of 1st chart row, k11(18)A, seed st 6A.

2nd row Seed st 6A, p11(18)A, p across 41 sts of 2nd chart row, p11(18)A, seed st 6A.

These 2 rows **set** the position of the chart and continue seed st and St st to each side.

Working correct chart rows (with white sts worked in appropriate background color), cont until all 79 chart rows have been worked.

Cont in A only, work 15(21) rows.

SHAPE NECK

Next row (right side) Seed st 6, k21, bind off center 21(35) sts, patt to end and cont on these 27 sts only, leaving rem 27 sts on a holder.

Next row Seed st 6, p to last 2 sts, p2tog.

Next row Bind off 2 sts, patt to end.

Rep these 2 rows 6 times more. *6 sts.*

Leave these 6 sts on a holder.

With wrong side facing, rejoin yarn to 27 sts on holder.

Next row Bind off 2 sts, patt to end.

Next row Patt to last 2 sts, k2tog.

Rep these 2 rows 6 times more. *6 sts.*

Next row Patt to end.

COLLAR

Pick-up row (right side) With size 3 (3.25mm) circular needle, seed st 6, pick up and k 63(77) sts evenly along neck edge, seed st 6 sts from holder, cast on 26 sts. *101(115) sts.*

With size 3 (3.25mm) needles and a spare length of A, cast on 26 sts and set aside.

With wrong side facing, return to 101(115) sts on circular needle, seed st to end, then seed st across 26 sts on needle. *127(141) sts.*

Work 11 rows in seed st.

Dec row Seed st 6, [p3tog, seed st 11] 8(9) times, p3tog, seed st 6. *109(121) sts.*

Work 11 rows in seed st.

Bind off in seed st.

CHEST STRAPS MAKE 2

With size 3 (3.25mm) needles and D, cast on 31 sts.

Work in seed st as for coat until strap measures 2¼"/6cm.

Bind off in seed st.

TO FINISH

Lay the coat on your dog to determine where to position the straps, then sew in place.

Cut the piece of hook-and-loop fastener in half. Sew one hook piece to the wrong side of one end of the collar and one loop piece to the right side of the other end of the collar. Sew one hook piece to the wrong side of one strap and one loop piece to the right side of the other strap.

Using duplicate stitch, embroider the diagonal lines and dog collar shown on the chart.

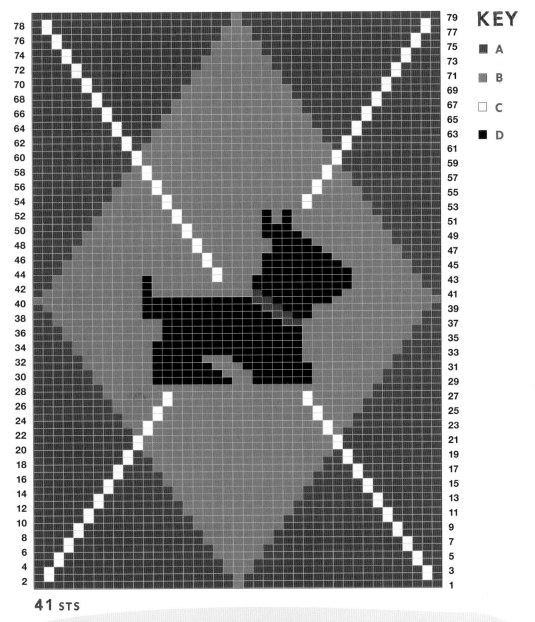

41 STS

CHART NOTES

When working from this chart, work all odd-numbered right-side rows from right to left in knit stitch and work all even-numbered wrong-side rows from left to right in purl stitch. Work the stitches in either yarn A, B, C, or D as appropriate. This color motif is worked using the intarsia method. Use separate strands or small balls of yarn for each color area and then twist them together where they meet to prevent a gap from forming. Using duplicate stitch, embroider the diagonal lines and dog collar on completion.

HIGHLAND HOUND

HIGHLAND HOUND

A touch of ancestral tartan never looks out of place when a dog is roamin' in the gloamin'. Tartan isn't only the preserve of the Gordon Setter and the Cairn Terrier, every breed of pooch can wear the Dog-las tartan.

SIZES

Two sizes small/medium (medium/large)—see coat measurements below and pages 8 and 9 to determine which size suits your dog

Measurements of knitted coat

Length measured along back 13¼(15½)"/33.5(39.5)cm

Width measured around chest (excluding straps) 12½(14¾)"/31.5(37.5)cm

Note: Measurements given in the instructions are adjustable depending on your dog.

MATERIALS

2(3) x 1¾oz (50g) balls of Debbie Bliss Blue Faced Leicester Aran (100% wool, aran-weight) in each of red (A) and navy (B) approx 164(246)yd/150(225)m each

Pair each of sizes 7 and 8 (4.5mm and 5mm) knitting needles

Piece of black hook-and-loop fastener, 4"/10cm by 2"/5cm, and matching sewing thread

GAUGES

20 sts and 22 rows to 4"/10cm square over main patt using size 8 (5mm) needles and 20 sts and 42 rows to 4"/10cm square over garter st using size 7 (4.5mm) needles.

ABBREVIATIONS

See page 13.

COAT

With size 7 (4.5mm) needles and A, cast on 63(75) sts.

K 5 rows.

Change to 5mm US 8) needles.

Work from chart as follows:

1st row (right side) K3A, k across 57(69) sts of 1st chart row, k3A.

2nd row K3A, p across 57(69) sts of 2nd chart row, k3A.

These 2 rows set the St st chart with garter st edges.

Work 50(62) rows more, ending with a wrong-side row.

SHAPE NECK

Next row (right side) Patt 24, bind off center 15(27) sts, patt to end and cont on these 24 sts only, leaving rem sts on a holder.

Next row Patt to end.

Next row Bind off 2 sts, patt to end.

Rep these 2 rows 5 times more.

Next row Patt to end.

Leave these 12 sts on a holder.

With wrong side facing, rejoin yarn to 24 sts on first holder, bind off 2 sts, patt to end.

Next row Patt to end.

Next row Bind off 2 sts, patt to end.

Rep the last 2 rows 4 times more. *12 sts.*

Patt 2 rows.

COLLAR

Pick-up row (right side) With A, k12, pick up and k 38(50) sts around bound-off edge, k 12 sts from holder. *62(74) sts.*

Cont with size 7 (4.5mm) needles and A only.

Next row Cast on 22(27) sts, k these 22(27) cast-on sts, then k62(74).

Next row Cast on 22(27) sts, k to end. *106(128) sts.*

K 13 rows.

Dec row K6(8), [skp, k2tog, k6(8)] 10 times. *86(108) sts.*

K 8 rows.

Bind off.

CHEST STRAPS MAKE 2

With size 7 (4.5mm) needles and A, cast on 36 sts.

Work in garter st (k every row) until strap measures 2¼"/6cm from cast-on edge.

Bind off.

TO FINISH

Lay the coat on your dog to determine where to position the straps, then sew them in place.

Cut the piece of hook-and-loop fastener in half. Sew one hook piece to the wrong side of one end of the collar and one loop piece to the right side of the other end of the collar. Sew one hook piece to the wrong side of one strap and one loop piece to the right side of the other strap.

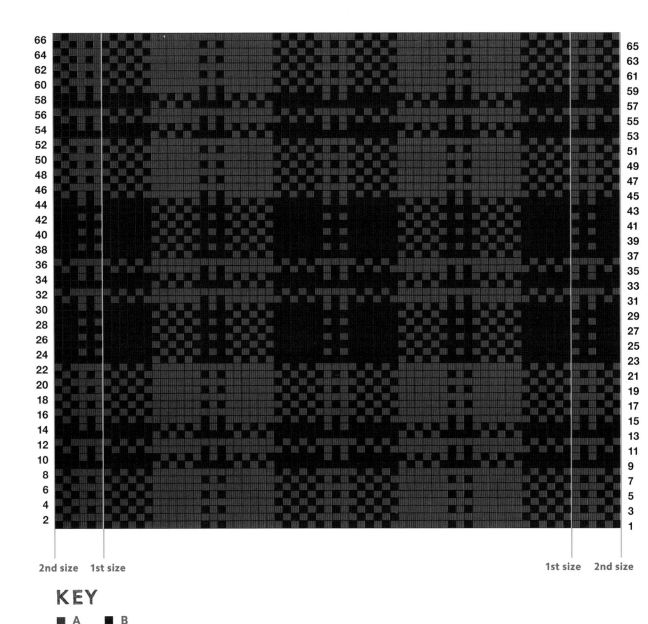

Row numbers left side (bottom to top): 2, 4, 6, 8, 10, 12, 14, 16, 18, 20, 22, 24, 26, 28, 30, 32, 34, 36, 38, 40, 42, 44, 46, 48, 50, 52, 54, 56, 58, 60, 62, 64, 66

Row numbers right side (bottom to top): 1, 3, 5, 7, 9, 11, 13, 15, 17, 19, 21, 23, 25, 27, 29, 31, 33, 35, 37, 39, 41, 43, 45, 47, 49, 51, 53, 55, 57, 59, 61, 63, 65

2nd size   1st size   1st size   2nd size

KEY

■ A   ■ B

CHART NOTES

When working from this chart, work all odd-numbered right-side rows from right to left
in knit stitch and work all even-numbered wrong-side rows from left to right in purl stitch.
Work the stitches in either yarn A or yarn B as appropriate. The basic pattern is stripes.
When working the navy vertical stripes, use separate small balls of yarn for each stripe
and carry the yarn up on the wrong side of the work. When working the spot pattern, use
small amounts of contrasting color for each block of spots.

GOOD-BOY GANSEY

In this denim-look cabled coat, any dog will be the catch of the day. A traditional seafarers' sweater, the classic gansey is especially suited to water dogs.

SIZES

Two sizes small/medium (medium/large)—see coat measurements below and pages 8 and 9 to determine which size suits your dog

Measurements of knitted coat

Length measured along back 13½(15¾)"/34(40)cm

Width measured around chest 20(22)"/51(55.5)cm

MATERIALS

3(4) x 1¾oz (50g) balls Debbie Bliss Blue Faced Leicester Aran
(100% wool, aran-weight) in denim approx 246(328)yd/225(300)m

Pair each of sizea 6 and 8 (4mm and 5mm) knitting needles

Set of four size 7 (4.5mm) double-pointed knitting needles

Cable needle

GAUGE

18 sts and 24 rows to 4"/10cm square over St st using size 8 (5mm) needles.

ABBREVIATIONS

C4F slip next 2 sts onto cable needle and hold to front of work,
k2, then k2 from cable needle.

Also see page 13.

PATTERN PANEL
WORKED OVER 11 STS

1st row K to end.

2nd row P to end.

3rd row K to end.

4th row K to end.

5th row K to end.

6th row K to end.

7th row K to end.

8th row P5, k1, p5.

9th row K4, p1, k1, p1, k4.

10th row P3, [k1, p1] twice, k1, p3.

11th row K2, [p1, k1] 3 times, p1, k2.

12th row P3, [k1, p1] twice, k1, p3.

13th row K4, p1, k1, p1, k4.

14th row P5, k1, p5.

15th–26th rows Rep 3rd to 14th rows.

These 26 rows complete the center panel.

BACK

** With size 6 (4mm) needles, cast on 46(50) sts.

K 3 rows.

Rib row [K1, p1] to end.

Rep the last row 8(12) times more and inc one st in center of last row. *47(51) sts.*

K 3 rows **.

Change to size 8 (5mm) needles.

Now work in patt as follows:

1st row (right side) [P1, k1] 1(2) times, p1, k6, p1, k6, p1, k1, work across 11 sts of 1st row of patt panel, k1, p1, k6, p1, k6, p1, [k1, p1] 1(2) times.

2nd row [P1, k1] 2(3) times, [p4, k1, p1, k1] twice, work across 11 sts of 2nd row of patt panel, [k1, p1, k1, p4] twice, [k1, p1] 2(3) times.

3rd row [P1, k1] 2(3) times, [C4F, k1, p1, k1] twice, work across 11 sts of 3rd row of patt panel, [k1, p1, k1, C4F] twice, [k1, p1] 2(3) times.

4th row [P1, k1] 2(3) times, [p4, k1, p1, k1] twice, work across 11 sts of 4th row of patt panel, [k1, p1, k1, p4] twice, [k1, p1] 2(3) times.

These 4 rows **set** the patt panel and **form** the cable panels and seed st at each side.

5th–26th rows Cont in patt to end of 26th row.

27th row [P1, k1] 2(3) times, [C4F, k1, p1, k1] twice, k11, [k1, p1, k1, C4F] twice, [k1, p1] 2(3) times.

28th row [P1, k1] 2(3) times, [p4, k1, p1, k1] twice, p11, [k1, p1, k1, p4] twice, [k1, p1] 2(3) times.

P 4 rows.

Beg with a k row, work in St st until Back measures 12(14)"/30(35)cm from cast-on edge, ending with a p row.

SHAPE LOWER BACK

Next row K2, skp, k to last 4 sts, k2tog, k2.

Next row P to end.

Rep the last 2 rows 1(2) times more. *43(45) sts.*

Leave these sts on a holder.

FRONT

Work as given for Back until 16 rows have been worked in patt, so ending with a wrong-side row.

Keeping the patt to match Back, shape as follows:

SHAPE FOR LEGHOLES

Bind off 8(9) sts at beg of next 2 rows. *31(33) sts.*

Work 14 rows more.

Cast on 8(9) sts at beg of next 2 rows. *47(51) sts.*

Work even until 12 rows fewer have been worked than on Back to lower back shaping.

SHAPE LOWER EDGE

Next row (right side) K14, turn and work on these sts only for first side of shaping, leaving rem sts on a spare needle.

Dec one st at inside edge on next 11 rows. *3 sts.* Bind off.

With right side facing, slip 19(23) sts at center onto a holder, rejoin yarn to rem 14 sts, k to end.

Dec one st at inside edge on next 11 rows. *3 sts.* Bind off.

LOWER EDGING

Sew right side seam (from cast-on edges to beginning of lower back shaping), leaving leghole edge open.

With right side facing and size 6 (4mm) needles, pick up and k 12 sts down left front shaped edge, k across 19(23) sts at center front, pick up and k 12 sts up right front shaped ege, 4(8) sts up shaped edge of back, k across 43(45) sts at lower back, pick up and k 4(8) sts down shaped edge of back. *94(108) sts.*

Rib row [K1, p1] to end.

Rep the last row 4 times more.

Bind off in rib.

LEGHOLE EDGINGS

Sew left side seam, leaving leghole edge open.

With right side facing and size 7 (4.5mm) double-pointed needles, pick up and k 38(46) sts evenly around leg opening.

Arrange sts over three of the needles.

Rib round [K1, p1] to end.

Rib 3 rounds more.

Bind off in rib.

SCRUM HOUND

Whether they're a fly half or a prop forward, it's a certainty that your dog will occupy the Number 1 position in the home team. Customize this sports shirt by making it in your own favorite team colors, that way you're bound to score a try.

SIZE

One size medium/large—see coat measurements below and pages 8 and 9 to determine if this size suits your dog

Measurements of knitted coat

Length measured along back 21¾"/55cm

Width measured around chest 22"/56cm

MATERIALS

Three 1¾oz (50g) balls of Rialto DK (100% Merino Wool, double-knitting-weight) in claret (A) approx 345yd/315m, two 1¾oz (50g) balls in blue (B), approx 230yd/210m one 1¾oz (50g) ball in white (C) approx 115yd/105m and a small amount in red (D)

Pair of size 6 (4mm) knitting needles

size 6 (4mm) circular knitting needle, 31½"/80cm long

Set of four size 3 (3.25mm) double-pointed knitting needles

GAUGE

22 sts and 30 rows to 4"/10cm square over St st using size 6 (4mm) needles.

ABBREVIATIONS

See page 13.

COAT WORKED ALL IN ONE

With size 6 (4mm) needles and A, cast on 87 sts.

1st rib row (right side) K1, [p1, k1] to end.

2nd rib row P1, [k1, p1] to end.

Rep the last 2 rows until rib measures 2¼"/ 6cm, ending with a 2nd rib row.

Change to size 6 (4mm) circular needle.

Work backward and forward in St st rows of 16 rows B, 16 rows A throughout and **at the same time** keeping stripe sequence correct, shape as follows:

1st row (right side) Kfb, k to last 2 sts, kfb, k1.

2nd row Pfb, p to last 2 sts, pfb, p1.

3rd row K to end.

4th row Pfb, p to last 2 sts, pfb, p1.

5th row Kfb, k to last 2 sts, kfb, k1.

6th row P to end.

Rep these 6 rows 3 times more, then 1st to 3rd rows again. *123 sts.*

Next row P to end.

DIVIDE FOR LEGHOLES

Next row With size 6 (4mm) needles, k11, turn and cont on these sts only, leaving rem sts on the circular needle.

Cont in St st and work 2¼"/5.5cm, ending with a k row.

Leave sts on first holder.

With right side facing, slip 12 sts from circular needle onto second holder, rejoin yarn to rem 100 sts, k to last 23 sts, turn and cont on these 77 sts only, leaving rem 23 sts on the circular needle.

Beg with a p row, work 2¼"/5.5cm in St st, ending with a k row (the same number of rows should be worked as first section), leave sts on third holder.

With right side facing, slip 12 sts from circular needle onto fourth holder, rejoin yarn to rem 11 sts, k to end.

Beg with a p row, work 2¼"/5.5cm in St st, ending with a k row (the same number of rows should be worked as first section).

Do not cut off yarn.

With wrong side facing work as follows:

Joining row (wrong side) P11, cast on 12 sts, p 77 sts from third holder, cast on 12 sts, p 11 sts from first holder. *123 sts.*

Beg with a k row, work 6 rows in St st.

Next row (right side) K45, k across 32 sts of 1st row of chart, k46.

Next row P46, p across 32 sts of 2nd row of chart, p45.

These 2 rows set the position of the chart.

Working correct chart rows and stripe sequence, cont until the 3rd stripe in B has been worked, so ending with a p row.

SHAPE LOWER BACK

Cont to work chart until all 49 rows have been worked and **at the same time**, shape as follows:

*** Bind off 8 sts at beg of next 2 rows. *107 sts.*

Next row K 1, skp, k to last 3 sts, k2tog, k1.

Next row P to end.

Rep the last 2 rows until 55 sts rem.

Work even until work measures 8¾"/22cm from ***, ending with a p row.

Leave sts on a holder.

LOWER EDGING

With right side facing, size 6 (4mm) circular needle, and A, beg at *** and pick up and k 8 sts across bound-off sts, 56 sts up shaped right-hand edge of back, k across 55 sts from back holder, pick up and k 56 sts down shaped left-hand edge of back, then 8 sts of across bound-off sts. *183 sts.*

Beg with a 2nd rib row, work 7 rows in rib.

Bind off in rib.

LEGHOLE EDGINGS

With right side facing and size 6 (4mm) double-pointed needles, k across 12 sts held on second holder, pick up and k 14 sts up row-ends of leg edge, 12 sts across cast-on edge, then 14 sts down row-ends of rem leg edge. *52 sts.*

Arrange sts over three of the needles.

Rib round [K1, p1] 26 times.

Rep rib round 5 times more.

Bind off in rib.

Rep for rem leghole edging, working across 12 sts on fourth holder.

TO FINISH

Sew underbelly seam, from cast-on neck edge to bound-off back edge, taking a half stitch from each side into the seam.

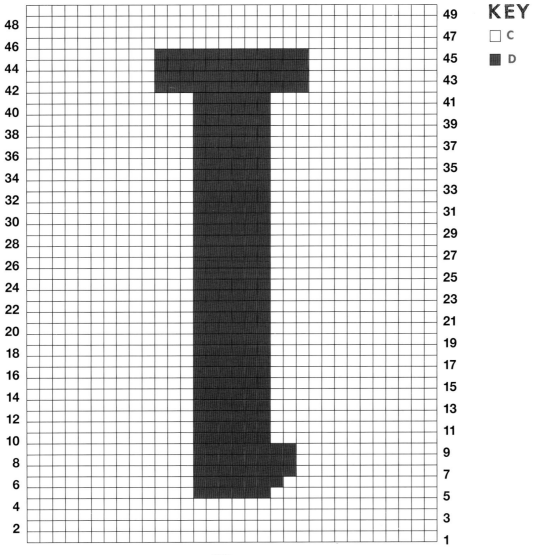

32 STS

CHART NOTES

When working from this chart, work all odd-numbered right-side rows from right to left in knit stitch and work all even-numbered wrong-side rows from left to right in purl stitch. Work the stitches in either yarn C or yarn D as appropriate. This color motif is worked using the intarsia method. Use separate strands or small balls of yarn for each color area and then twist them together where they meet to prevent a gap from forming.

FAIR ISLE FURBABY

With its origins in the remote Shetland Isles beyond the north of Scotland, this Fair Isle colorwork coat will keep country dogs cozy even in the coldest of weather. Topped off with a matching bonnet, known as a tam-o'-shanter, your dog sure will look bonnie.

SIZES

Two sizes small/medium (medium/large)—see coat measurements below and pages 8 and 9 to determine which size suits your dog

Measurements of knitted coat

Length measured along back 15(17¼)"/38(43.5)cm

Width measured around chest 17¾(22¾)"/45(57.5)cm

MATERIALS

One 1¾oz (50g) ball of Debbie Bliss Baby Cashmerino (55% wool, 33% microfiber, 12% cashmere; fine-weight) in each of eight colors—forest green (A), red (B), yellow (C), light green (D), duck egg (E), gray (F), ecru (G), and pale pink (H) approx 136yd/125m each

Pair each of sizes 2 and 3 (3mm and 3.25mm) knitting needles

Set of four size 3 (3.25mm) double-pointed knitting needles

Length of black shirring elastic

GAUGE

25 sts and 30 rows to 4"/10cm over patt using size 3 (3.25mm) needles.

ABBREVIATIONS

See page 13.

NOTES

✂ Shirring elastic can be threaded around the neck edge of the coat for a snug fit.

✂ If you make the coat you should have sufficient yarn remaining to work the beret.

✂ When working the beret, carry A up the side edge rather than cutting the yarn.

BACK OF COAT

With size 2 (3mm) needles and A, cast on 57(73) sts.

K 6 rows.

P 1 row.

Change to size 3 (3.25mm) needles and work from chart as follows:

1st row (right side) K3A, [k across 1st row of 16-st patt rep] 3(4) times, work last 3 sts of chart, k3A.

2nd row K3A, p first 3 sts of chart, [p across 2nd row of 16-st patt rep] 3(4) times, k3A.

These 2 rows **set** the patt with garter st edging.

Work to end of 80th chart row, then work chart rows 1 to 25(41) again.

Change to size 2 (3mm) needles and work in A only.

Next row K3, p to last 3 sts, k3.

K 5 rows. Bind off.

FRONT OF COAT

Work as given for Back until 34(42) rows have been worked in patt.

SHAPE FOR LEGHOLES

Bind off 12(16) sts at beg of next 2 rows. *33(41) sts.*

Work 18(24) rows more.

Cast on 12(16) sts at beg of next 2 rows. *57(73) sts.*

Cont in patt to end of 80th chart row, then work chart rows 1 to 3(19) again.

Change to size 2 (3mm) needles and work in A only.

Next row K3, p to last 3 sts, k3.

K 5 rows. Bind off.

LEGHOLE EDGINGS

Sew side seams, leaving leghole edges open.

With right side facing, size 3 (3.25mm) double-pointed needles, and A, pick up and k 48(60) sts around each leghole edge.

Arrange sts over three of the needles.

1st round [K1, p1] to end.

Work 3(5) rounds more in rib.

Bind off loosely in rib.

BERET

With size 3 (3.25mm) needles and A, cast on 64 sts.

K 3 rows.

Next row (right side) K5, [M1, k1, M1, k8] 6 times, M1, k1, M1, k4. *78 sts.*

K 1 row.

With B, k 1 row.

Next row (wrong side) With B, k6, [M1, k1, M1, k10] 6 times, M1, k1, M1, k5. *92 sts.*

With A, k 2 rows.

With C, k 1 row.

Next row With C, k7, [M1, k1, M1, k12] 6 times, M1, k1, M1, k6. *106 sts.*

With E, k 2 rows.

With A, k 2 rows.

With H, k 1 row.

Next row With H, k6, [k2tog, k1, skp, k10] 6 times, k2tog, k1, skp, k5. *92 sts.*

With A, k 2 rows.

With F, k 1 row.

Next row With F, k5, [k2tog, k1, skp, k8] 6 times, k2tog, k1, skp, k4. *78 sts.*

With A, k 2 rows.

With D, k 1 row.

Next row With D, k4, [k2tog, k1, skp, k6] 6 times, k2tog, k1, skp, k3. *64 sts.*

With A, k 2 rows.

With B, k 1 row.

Next row With B, k3, [k2tog, k1, skp, k4] 6 times, k2tog, k1, skp, k2. *50 sts.*

With A, k 2 rows.

With C, k 1 row.

Next row With C, k2, [k2tog, k1, skp, k2] 6 times, k2tog, k1, skp, k1. *36 sts.*

With A, k 2 rows.

With E, k 1 row.

Next row K1, [k2tog, k1, skp] 6 times, k2tog k1, skp. *22 sts.*

With A, k 1 row.

Next row With A, k1, [k3tog] 7 times. *8 sts.*

Cut off yarn, thread through rem sts, pull to gather, and secure.

Sew beret seam.

Make a pompom 2"/5cm in diameter from remaining yarn and sew to top of beret.

Attach a length of shirring elastic to the beret to keep it in place on your dog's head.

CHART NOTES

When working from this chart, work all odd-numbered right-side rows from right to left in knit stitch and work all even-numbered wrong-side rows from left to right in purl stitch; when knitting from this chart, work the stitches in either yarn A, B, C, D, E, F, G, or H as appropriate. This color motif is worked using the stranding method. Carry the yarn not in use across the wrong side of the work, weaving in where it crosses more than 3 stitches.

KEY

- ■ A
- ■ B
- □ C
- □ D
- ■ E
- ■ F
- □ G
- ■ H

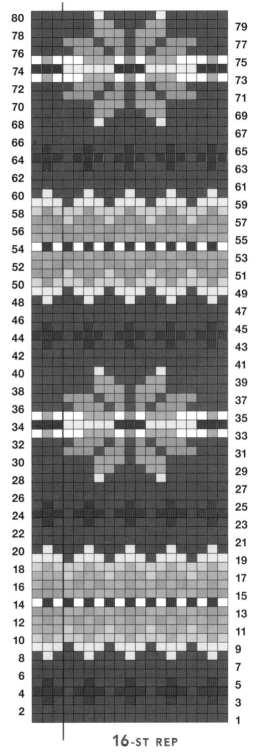

16-ST REP

PARKA BARKER

This cool khaki coat with its fur-lined hood is the ultimate in city dog wear. When catching up with wee-mails at the nearest lamppost, no self-respecting streetwise mutt would be caught dressed anything else.

SIZES

Two sizes small/medium (medium/large)—see coat measurements below and pages 8 and 9 to determine which size suits your dog

Measurements of knitted coat

Length measured along back 14¼(18¼)"/36(46)cm

Width measured around chest 17¼(21¼)"/44(54)cm

MATERIALS

Three 1¾oz (50g) balls of Debbie Bliss Rialto Chunky (100% merino wool, chunky-weight) in olive (A) approx 195yd/180m

One 1¾oz (50g) ball of Louisa Harding Luzia (80% viscose, 20% nylon; super-bulky-weight) in otter (B) approx 43 yards

Small amount of Debbie Bliss Rialto DK (100% merino wool, double-knitting-weight) in dark green (C)

Pair of size 10½ (6.5mm) knitting needles

Size 10½ (6.5mm) circular knitting needle

Two size 6 (4mm) double-pointed knitting needles

One button

GAUGE

15 sts and 21 rows to 4"/10cm square over St st using size 10½ (6.5mm) needles.

ABBREVIATIONS

See page 13.

BACK

With size 10½ (6.5mm) needles and A, cast on 33(41) sts.

1st row K1, [p1, k1] to end.

2nd row P1, [k1, p1] to end.

Rep the last 2 rows once more.

Beg with a k row, work in St st until Back measures 14¼(18¼)"/36(46)cm from cast-on edge.

Leave sts on a holder.

FRONT

Work exactly as given for Back until Front measures 12¾(16¼)"/32(41)cm from cast-on edge, ending with a p row.

SHAPE LOWER EDGE

Next row K9(12) sts, turn and cont on these sts only for first side, leaving rem sts on spare needle.

Dec one st at inside edge of next 7(10) rows. *2 sts.*

Bind off.

With right side facing, slip first 15(17) sts onto a holder, rejoin yarn to rem 9(12) sts.

Dec one st at inside edge of next 7(10) rows. *2 sts.*

Bind off.

HOOD

With size 10½ (6.5mm) needles and A, cast on 44(52) sts.

Beg with a k row, work in St st until hood measures 11¾(13¾)"/30(35)cm from cast-on edge.

Bind off.

Fold the bound-off edge in half and sew the seam to form the top of hood.

With right side facing and B, pick up and k 120 sts along the row-ends of the hood and work in garter st (k every row) for approximately 1½"/4cm.

Bind off.

CORD

With size 6 (4mm) double-pointed needles and C, cast on 5 sts.

Use two double-pointed needles to work cord as follows:

K 1 row.

Next row Slip all 5 sts to other end of needle, pull the yarn tightly from the last st and k 5 sts.

Rep the last row, so forming a tube, until cord measures approximately 22"/56cm.

Bind off.

FALSE POCKET

With size 10½ (6.5mm) needles and A, cast on 15 sts.

K 1 row.

Next row (right side) K to end.

Next row K1, p to last st, k1.

Rep the last 2 rows twice more.

1st dec row K1, skp, k to last 3 sts, k2tog, k1.

2nd dec row K1, p2tog tbl, p to last 3 sts, p2tog, k1.

Rep the last 2 rows, until 5 sts rem.

Next row K1, p3tog, k1.

Bind off rem 3 sts.

LOWER EDGING

Sew the side seams, leaving a gap of 4¾(5½)"/12(14)cm in the seam, approximately 2¾(3¼)"/7(8)cm down from cast-on edge for legholes.

With size 10½ (6.5mm) circular needle, pick up and k 8(12) sts down right front shaped edge, k across 15(17) sts on holder, pick up and k 8(12) sts up left front shaped edge, then k across 33(41) sts on back holder. *64(82) sts.*

Rib round [K1, p1] to end.

Rib 1 round more.

Bind off loosely in rib.

TO FINISH

Sew the cast-on edge of the hood inside of the neck edge behind the last rib row, leaving a space of approximately 5½"/14cm at center front.

Beg at center front, thread the cord through the rib at the cast-on end of coat (neck edge), ending at center front, then stitch the cord in place at intervals behind the ribbing.

Tie a knot at each end of the cord.

Slipstitch the false pocket to back, approximately 8¾"/22cm up from cast-on edge.

Sew the button onto the pocket.

DEPUTY
DOG

DEPUTY DOG

When patrolling the borders of Dog County, a Deputy Sheriff needs to look distinguished. This smart button-up vest, accessorized with a star-shaped badge, imparts the authority on any dog to run out undesirables to keep the peace.

SIZES

Two sizes small/medium (medium/large)—see coat measurements below and pages 8 and 9 to determine which size suits your dog

Measurements of knitted coat

Length measured along back approximately 12(13¾)"/30.5(35)cm

Width measured around chest 17¾(20½)"/45(52)cm

MATERIALS

3(4) x 1¾oz (50g) balls of Debbie Bliss Blue Faced Leicester Aran (100% wool, aran-weight) in chocolate (A) approx 246(328)yd/225(300)m and small amount in mustard (B)

Pair of size 8 (5mm) knitting needles

Set of four size 7 (4.50mm) double-pointed knitting needles

Three small buttons

GAUGE

18 sts and 24 rows to 4"/10cm square over St st using size 8 (5mm) needles.

ABBREVIATIONS

M1pw make one purlwise.

Also see page 13.

COAT WORKED ALL IN ONE

RIGHT SIDE OF COAT

With size 8 (5mm) needles and A, cast on 2 sts.
P 1 row.

Next row Cast on 3 sts, k to last st, M1, k1.

Next row P1, M1pw, p to end.

Rep the last 2 rows 5 times more. *32 sts.*

Next row Cast on 6(12) sts, k to end.
38(44) sts.

Next row P to end.

Leave these sts on a spare needle.

LEFT SIDE OF COAT

With size 8 (5mm) needles and A, cast on 2 sts.
K 1 row.

Next row Cast on 3 sts, p to last st, M1pw, k1.

Next row K1, M1, k to end.

Rep the last 2 rows 5 times more. *32 sts.*

Next row Cast on 6(12) sts, p to end.
38(44) sts.

Joining row K38(44) sts, from left side, then
k 38(44) sts from right side. *76(88) sts.*

Mark the center and each end of last row with
colored threads.

Cont in St st until coat measures 3¼(4½)"/
8(11)cm from markers, ending with a p row.

DIVIDE FOR LEGHOLES

Next row K19(22) and turn, leaving rem sts
unworked.

Work 12 rows on these 19(22) sts.

Leave these 19(22) sts on first holder.

With right side facing, rejoin yarn to rem
57(66) sts, bind off 9(11) sts, with 1 st on
needle after bind-off, k next 19(21) sts, turn
and work 12 rows on these 20(22) sts.

Leave these 20(22) sts on second holder.

With right side facing, rejoin yarn to rem
27(32) sts, bind off 9(11) sts, k to end.

Work 12 rows on these 19(22) sts.

Joining row P19(22), cast on 9(11) sts,
p20(22) from second holder, cast on 9(11) sts,
p19(22) from first holder. *76(88) sts.*

SHAPE FOR V-NECK

Next row K2, skp, k to last 4 sts, k2tog, k2.

Next row P to end.

Rep the last 2 rows 9(11) times more. *56(64)
sts.*

Leave these sts on a spare needle.

LEGHOLE EDGINGS

With right side facing, size 7 (4.5mm) double-
pointed needles and A, pick up and k 42(46) sts
around leghole edge.

Arrange sts over three of the needles.

Rib row [K1, p1] to end.

Rep the last row 4 times more.

Bind off in rib.

LEFT BAND AND COLLAR

With right side facing, size 7 (4.5mm) needles,
and A, cast on one stitch, pick up and k 25(31)
sts along edge from marker at center of left
and right side joining row to "point," one st
at point (mark this st with a colored thread),
13 sts along edge to corner, one st at corner
(mark this st with a colored thread), 25(30)
sts up straight edge of back to beg of neck
shaping, 23(26) sts along shaped neck edge,
k the first 28(32) from spare needle, cast on
one st. *118(136) sts.*

1st and 2nd row [P1, k1] 14(16) times, turn
[p1, k1] to end.

The last 2 rows set the rib.

Next 2 rows Rib 30(34), turn, rib to end.

Next 2 rows Rib 32(36), turn, rib to end.

Cont in this way, working 2 more sts into rib until 46(50) sts have been worked in rib, turn, rib to end.

Next row Rib 38(42), turn and work on these sts only.

Rib 9 rows more.

Bind off in rib.

Rejoin yarn to inner edge of rem sts, M1, rib 10, turn, rib to end.

Next row Rib to end.

Next row [Rib to marked st, M1, k1 (marked st), M1] twice, rib to end.

Rep the last 2 rows twice more and the first row again.

Bind off in rib, inc as before.

RIGHT BAND AND COLLAR

With right side facing, size 7 (4.5mm) needles, and A, cast on one st, k28(32) from spare needle, pick up and k 23(26) sts along shaped neck edge to beg of neck shaping, 25(30) sts down straight edge of back to corner, one st at corner (mark this st with a colored thread), 13 sts to "point," one st at point (mark this st with a colored thread), then 25(31) sts to center front, cast on one st. *118(136) sts.*

Next row [P1, k1] to end.

The last row sets the rib.

Next 2 rows Rib 28(32), turn rib to end.

Next 2 rows Rib 30(34), turn, rib to end.

Next 2 rows Rib 32(36), turn, rib to end.

Cont in this way, working 2 more sts into rib until 46(50) sts have been worked in rib, turn, rib to end.

Next row Rib 38(42), turn and work on these sts.

Work 8 rows more in rib.

Bind off in rib.

Rejoin yarn to inner edge of rem sts, cast on one st, rib 10, turn rib to end.

Next row [Rib to marked st, M1, k1 (marked st), M1] twice, rib to end.

Next row Rib to end.

Buttonhole row Rib 15, [rib 2tog, yo, rib 8(10)] twice, rib 2tog, yo, [rib to marked st, M1, k1 (marked st), M1] twice, rib to end.

Next row Rib to end.

Next row [Rib to marker, M1, k1, M1] twice, rib to end.

Next row Rib to end.

Bind off in rib, inc as before.

TO FINISH

Using duplicate stitch and B, embroider the star motif on the right back following the chart.

Sew together row-end edges of collar and band.

Sew on buttons.

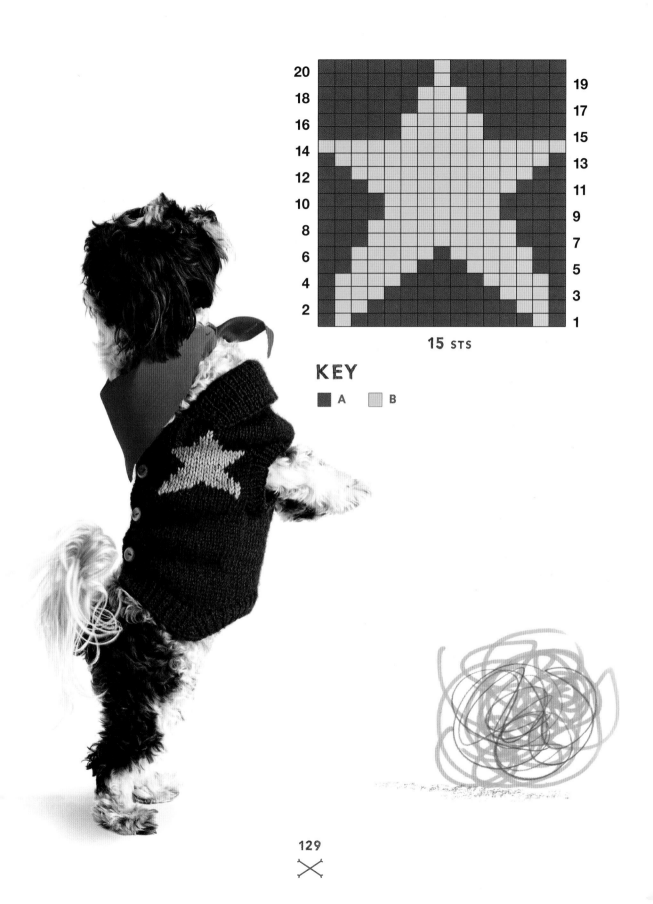

20																19
18																17
16																15
14																13
12																11
10																9
8																7
6																5
4																3
2																1

15 STS

KEY

A   B

PIERROT HAT AND RUFF

PIERROT HAT AND RUFF

The inherent innocence and natural comic timing of all dogs means they are perfectly cast to act the clown. You may find that out of all the knits in this book, the Pierrot Pooch is your dog's favorite. Just ask him what he wants to wear and he's sure to answer "Ruff."

SIZE

One size ruff is 24"/60cm in diameter—to fit all breeds, simply wrap the ruff either once or twice around your dog's neck

MATERIALS

Two 1¾oz (50g) balls of Debbie Bliss Rialto 4ply (100% extra fine merino wool, super-fine-weight) in white (A) approx 392yd/360m and one 1¾oz (50g) ball in black (B) approx 196yd/180m

Pair each of sizes 2 and 3 (3mm and 3.25mm) knitting needles

Size 3 (3.25mm) circular knitting needle

Length of black shirring elastic, for hat

Length of white shirring elastic, for ruff

GAUGE

28 sts and 36 rows to 4"/10cm square over St st using size 3 (3.25mm) needles.

ABBREVIATIONS

See page 13.

HAT PIECES MAKE 2

With size 3 (3.25mm) needles and A, cast on 42 sts.

Beg with a k row, work 26 rows in St st, so ending with a p row.

SHAPE TOP

Dec row K2, skp, k to last 4 sts, k2tog, k2.

Work 3 rows in St st.

Rep the last 4 rows until 12 sts rem, ending with a p row.

Dec row K2, skp, k to last 4 sts, k2tog, k2.
P 1 row.

Rep the last 2 rows once more. *8 sts.*

Next row K2, skp, k2tog, k2. *6 sts.*

Next row P2tog, p2, p2tog. *4 sts.*

Leave these sts on a safety pin.

Make second hat piece in same way, using B.

Place sts from both pins onto a needle.

Thread end through rem sts, pull to gather, and secure.

TO FINISH HAT

Sew both seams, reversing seams on last 20 rows at lower edge.

Roll the lower edge and stitch the roll in place at the sides.

Make a pompom 1½"/4cm in diameter in each color and attach to one seam.

Attach a length of black shirring elastic to the hat to keep it in place on your dog's head.

RUFF

With size 2 (3mm) needles and A, cast on 113 sts.

1st row P1, [k1, p1] to end.

2nd row K1, [p1, k1] to end.

These 2 rows form the rib.

Rib 6 rows more.

Change to size 3 (3.25mm) circular needle and work backward and forward in rows as follows:

Beg with a k row, work 2 rows in St st.

Inc row K1, [M1, k1] to end. *225 sts.*

Work 3 rows.

Inc row K1, [M1, k2] to end. *337 sts.*

Work 3 rows.

Inc row K1, [M1, k3] to end. *449 sts.*

Work 5 rows.

Inc row K1, [M1, k4] to end. *561 sts.*

Work 7 rows.

Change to B.

K 3 rows.

Bind off.

Sew the seam.

Run a length of white shirring elastic around the ribbed cast-on edge and around the first row of St st.

SANTA'S LITTLE HELPER

SANTA'S LITTLE HELPER

Every Christmas Eve, Santa's faithful helpers assist in spreading a little festive cheer. While presents are being delivered via chimneys across the land, the faithful canine companion of Santa Claus keeps tabs on all those puppies who have been naughty or nice.

SIZES

Two sizes small/medium (medium/large)—see coat measurements below and pages 8 and 9 to determine which size suits your dog

Measurements of knitted coat

Length measured along back 11½(13¼)"/29(34)cm

Width measured around chest (excluding straps) 11½(13¾)"/29(35)cm

Note: Measurements given in the instructions are adjustable depending on your dog.

MATERIALS

2(3) x 1¾oz (50g) balls of Debbie Bliss Blue Faced Leicester Aran (100% wool, aran-weight) in each of ecru (A) and red (B) approx 164 (246)yd/150 (225)m each, one 1¾oz (50g) ball in black (C) approx 82yd/75m, and a small amount in amber (D)

Pair each of sizes 6 and 7 (4mm and 4.5mm) knitting needles

Cable needle

Piece of hook-and-loop fastener, 2"/5cm square, in each of white and black and matching sewing threads

GAUGE

18 sts and 34 rows to 4"/10cm square over main patt using size 7 (4.5mm) needles.

ABBREVIATIONS

C4B slip next 2 sts onto cable needle and hold at back of work, k2, then k2 from cable needle.

C4F slip next 2 sts onto cable needle and hold to front of work, k2, then k2 from cable needle.

Tw2 insert right-hand needle into front of 2nd st on left-hand needle and k1, leave st on needle, then k first st on left-hand needle and slip both sts off needle together.

Also see page 13.

COAT

With size 7 (4.5mm) needles and A, cast on 58(70) sts.

1st row (right side) P to end.

2nd row K1, [p into front, back, and front of next st, k3tog] to last st, k1.

3rd row P to end.

4th row K1, [k3tog, p into front, back, and front of next st] to last st, k1.

These 4 rows form the blackberry patt and are repeated.

Work 8 rows more in patt.

Next row (right side) K10, slip these 10 sts onto first holder, cut off A, join on B, k18(24), k2tog, k18(24) and leave the last 10 sts on a second holder.

Work in main patt on center 37(49) sts as follows:

1st row (wrong side) P to end.

2nd row P2, [k1, p3] 8(11) times, k1, p2.

3rd row P37(49).

4th row K1, [p3, k1] 9(12) times.

These 4 rows form the patt and are repeated.

Cont in patt until work measures 9½(11½)"/ 24(29)cm from cast-on edge, ending with a wrong-side row.

SHAPE NECK

Next row (right side) Patt 14, bind off center 9(21) sts, patt to end.

Cont on 14 sts after bind-off as follows:

Next row Patt to end.

Next row Bind off 2 sts, patt to end.

Rep the last 2 rows 5 times more. *2 sts.*

Leave rem 2 sts on a holder.

With wrong side facing, rejoin yarn to rem 14 sts.

Next row Bind off 2 sts, patt to end.

Next row Patt to end.

Rep the last 2 rows 5 times more. *2 sts.*

Next row Patt to end.

Pick-up row (right side) K2, pick up and k 34(46) sts along bound-off edge, then k 2 sts from holder.

Leave these 38(50) sts on a holder.

LEFT SIDE EDGING

With right side facing and leaving a long yarn end, join A to 10 sts on second holder and cont in patt until edging fits up side of coat to neck edge, ending with a wrong-side row.

Leave these 10 sts on a holder.

RIGHT SIDE EDGING

With wrong side facing and leaving a long end, join A to 10 sts on first holder and cont in patt until edging fits up side of coat to neck edge, ending with a wrong-side row.

Do not cut off yarn.

COLLAR

Sew edgings in place.

With a spare length of A, cast on 20 sts and leave these sts on a spare needle.

With right side facing, return to right side edging, cast on 20 sts, p these 20 sts, p10 from right side edging, k38(50) from neck edge holder, p10 sts from left side edging, then p 20 cast-on sts from spare needle. *98(110) sts.*

Beg with a 2nd row, work 7 rows in blackberry st.

Change to size 6 (4mm) needles and work 4 rows more in patt.

Bind off.

BELT

Wth size 7 (4.5mm) needles and C, cast on 12 sts.

Foundation row (right side) P1, Tw2, p1, k4, p1, Tw2, p1.

Inc row P5, M1, p2, M1, p5. *14 sts.*

1st row P1, Tw2, p1, C4B, k2, p1, Tw2, p1.

2nd row P to end.

3rd row P1, Tw2, p1, k2, C4F, p1, Tw2, p1.

4th row P to end.

Rep the 1st–4th rows until belt measures approximately 26(30)in/66(76)cm, ending with a 1st row.

Bind off knitwise, working [k1, k2tog] twice across the central 6 cable sts.

BUCKLE

With size 6 (4mm) needles and D, cast on 40 sts.

1st row K to end.

2nd row K5, [M1, k1, M1, k9] 3 times, M1, k1, M1, k4. *48 sts.*

3rd row K5, [M1, k1, M1, k11] 3 times, M1, k1, M1, k6. *56 sts.*

4th row K7, [M1, k1, M1, k13] 3 times, M1, k1, M1, k6. *64 sts.*

Bind off and inc on this row as before.

Sew together the row-end edges.

PRONG

With size 6 (4mm) needles and D, cast on 17 sts.

P 1 row.

Bind off.

TO FINISH

Position the belt centrally on the coat. Then lay the coat on your dog to determine how far from the neck collar it needs to be and slipstitch in place.

Position the buckle over the center of the belt with the seam to one side and slipstitch in place. Attach the ends of the prong over the buckle seam.

Sew the hook section of the white piece of hook-and-loop fastener to the wrong side of one end of the collar and the loop section to the right side of the other end of the collar—you may need to adjust this positioning, depending on your dog. Sew the hook section of the black piece to the wrong side of one end of the belt and the loop section to the right side of the other end of the belt.

ACKNOWLEDGEMENTS

This book would not have been possible without the cooperation of our wonderful woofers and their accommodating owners. Thank you to all of them for turning up to our photoshoots so bright eyed and bushy tailed.

Brian & Ernie the Pugs with their mistress Clare; Buster the Schnauzer with his mistress Juliet; Carmel Corn the Teacup Yorkie with her mistress Tatiana; Coco the Cavalier King Charles Spaniel with her master Paul; Dexter the French Bulldog with his master Kian; Dudley the Bichon Frise with his mistress Jayne; Dulcie the Welsh Terrier with her mistress Ros; Elvis the Bedlington Terrier with her mistress Kate; Evie the Sporting Lucas Terrier with her mistress Grace; Floydy the Airedale Terrier with his mistress Elizabeth; George the Bulldog with his mistress Michelle; Ludo the Miniature English Bull Terrier with his master Nick; Millie the English Springer Spaniel with her mistress Sally; Ned & Henry the Miniature Dachshunds with their mistress Joy; Oscar the Schnauzer with his mistress Andrea; Oscar the Shih-Tzu x Yorkshire Terrier Cross with his mistress Sinéad; Pip & Bertie the Scottish Terriers with their mistress Heather; Pixie the French Bulldog with her mistress Ying; Smiffy the Parson Russell Terrier with his master Barry; Spider the Bichon Frise x Shih-Tzu Cross with her mistress Jade; William Wallace the Cockapoo with his mistress Victoria.

I would also like to say a big thank you to all the following:

To my wonderful commissioning editor Lisa Pendreigh, lover of all things canine, for her enthusiasm for the project and dreaming up the design concept.

To Arielle Gamble for art directing the photoshoots and so beautifully bringing together the whole design.

To the amazing illustrator Jo Clark for the delightful drawings that set the scene for our dog models.

To the brilliant photographer Richard Burns for the great dog portraits and coaxing the inner super model out of even the most reluctant pooch.

To Kevin, the owner of Studio 19, for his patience during the photoshoots and taking all the small puddles into his stride.

To Rosy Tucker who checked all the patterns, despite her misgivings! And to Sally Harding for giving everything an additional check.

To Penny Hill and her knitters who valiantly carried on when I couldn't knit fast enough.

Finally, to Jane O'Shea for giving the project the green light and Heather Jeeves, my agent, for all her hard work.

YARN DISTRIBUTORS

For stockists of Debbie Bliss yarns please contact:

UK & WORLDWIDE DISTRIBUTORS
Designer Yarns Ltd.
Units 8–10, Newbridge
Industrial Estate, Pitt Street,
Keighley, West Yorkshire
BD21 4PQ, UK
t: +44 (0) 1535 664222
enquiries@designeryarns.uk.com
www.designeryarns.uk.com

USA
Knitting Fever Inc.
315 Bayview Avenue,
Amityville, NY 11701, USA
t: +1 516 546 3600
www.knittingfever.com

**AUSTRALIA/
NEW ZEALAND**
Prestige Yarns Pty Ltd
Unit 6, 8–10 Pioneer Drive,
Bellambi, NSW 2518, Australia
t: +61 (0) 2 4285 6669
info@prestigeyarns.com
www.prestigeyarns.com

BRAZIL
Quatro Estacoes Com
Las Linhas e Acessorios Ltda
Av. Das Nacoes Unidas,
12551-9 Andar, Cep 04578-000
Sao Paulo, Brazil
t: +55 11 3443 7736
cristina@4estacoeslas.com.br

CANADA
Diamond Yarn Ltd
155 Martin Ross Avenue,
Unit 3, Toronto, Ontario

M3J 2L9, Canada
t: +1 416 736 6111
www.diamondyarn.com

DENMARK
Fancy Knit
Storegade, 13,8500 Grenaa,
Ramten, Denmark
t: +45 86 39 88 30
kelly@fancyknitdanmark.com

FINLAND
Eiran Tukku
Mäkelänkatu 54 B,
00510 Helsinki, Finland
t: +358 50 346 0575
maria.hellbom@eirantukku.fi

FRANCE
Plassard Diffusion
La Filature
71800 Varennes-sous-Dun,
France
t: +33 (0) 3 85282828
info@laines-plassard.com

**GERMANY/AUSTRIA/
SWITZERLAND/BENELUX**
**Designer Yarns
(Deutschland) GmbH**
Welserstrasse 10g,
D-51149 Köln,
Germany
t: +49 (0) 2203 1021910
info@designeryarns.de
www.designeryarns.de

HONG KONG
East Unity Company Ltd
Unit B2, 7/F Block B,
Kailey Industrial Centre,
12 Fung Zip Street, Chai Wan,
Hong Kong

t: +852 2869 7110
eastunity@yahoo.com.hk

HUNGARY
Sziget Store Kft
2310. Szigetszentmiklos,
Haszontalan dulo 34, Hungary
janosnemeth@mol.hu

ICELAND
Storkurinn ehf
Laugavegi 59, 101 Reykjavík,
Iceland
t: +354 551 8258
storkurinn@storkurinn.is

ITALY
Lucia Fornasari
Via Cuniberti, 22, Ivrea (TO),
Italy 10015
t: +0039 345 566 5568
info@lavoroamaglia.it
www.lavoroamaglia.it

KUWAIT
Agricultural Aquarium Co.
Shop No. 19, Rai Center, Al-Rai,
Kuwait 22002
t: +0965 66757 070
computerscience2003@gmail.com

MALAYSIA
Lily Handicraft
GF30, 31 Kompleks Yik Foong,
Jalan Laxamana, 30300 Ipoh
Perak, Malaysia
t: +0060 525 39036
yeohvivien@gmail.com

MEXICO
Estambres Crochet SA de CV
Aaron Saenz 1891-7,
Col. Santa Maria, Monterrey,

N.L. 64650, Mexico
t: +52 (81) 8335 3870
abremer@redmundial.com.mx

NORWAY
Viking of Norway
Bygdaveien 63, 4333 Oltedal,
Norway
t: +47 516 11 660
post@viking-garn.no
www.viking-garn.no

POLAND
AmiQs
Ul Michala Aniola 8, Bielawa
05-520 Konstancin Jeziorma,
Poland
t: +48 60 641 001
marcin@ittec.pl
www.amiqs.com

PORTUGAL
Knitting Labs
Rui Manuel Nunes Cardoso
Av Rainha D Leonor no 24,
2o dto, 1600-684 Lisbon
Portugal
t: +35 191 728 1659
luisa.arruda@knittinglabs.com
www.knittinglabs.com

RUSSIA
Golden Fleece Ltd.
Soloviyny Proezd 16
117593 Moscow,
Russian Federation,
Russia
t: +8 (903) 000 1967
levina@rukodelie.ru
www.rukodelie.ru

SINGAPORE
Quilts n Calicoes
163, Tanglin Road,
03-13, Tanglin Mall,
Singapore 247933
t: +65 6887 4708

quiltchick@quiltsncalicoes.com
www.quiltsncalicoes.com
quiltsncalicoes.blogspot.com

SPAIN
Oyambre Needlework SL
Balmes, 200 At. 4, 08006
Barcelona,
Spain
t: +34 (0) 93 487 26 72
info@oyambreonline.com

SOUTH KOREA
Ann Knitting
1402 14F, Dongjin Bldg,
735-6 Gyomun-dong, Guri-si,
Gyeonggi-do,
471-020 South Korea
t: +82 70 4367 2779
tedd@annknitting.com
www.annknitting.com'

SWEDEN
Nysta garn och textil
Hogasvagen 20,
S-131 47 Nacka, Sweden
t: +46 708 81 39 54
info@nysta.se
www.nysta.se

THAILAND
Needle World Co Ltd.
588 Pradit Manoontham Road,
Bangkok 10310, Thailand
t: +662 933 9167
needle-world.coltd@
googlemail.com

UKRAINE
**Zaremba Viktoriia
Volodymyrivna**
10v Mate Zalka Street,
Office 78
Kyiv 04 211,
Ukraine
t: +38 050 808 5423
pillara@rambler.ru

For more information on my
other books and yarns, please
visit www.debbieblissonline.com

Publishing Director Jane O'Shea
Commissioning Editor Lisa Pendreigh
Pattern Checkers Rosy Tucker & Sally Harding
Creative Director Helen Lewis
Designer Arielle Gamble
Illustrator Jo Clark
Photographer Richard Burns
Production Director Vincent Smith
Production Controller Sasha Hawkes

LARK
New York

An Imprint of Sterling Publishing
1166 Avenue of the Americas
New York, NY 10036

First published in 2014 by
Quadrille Publishing Limited

This Lark edition published in 2015
by Sterling Publishing

Text and project designs
© 2014 Debbie Bliss
Photography, illustration, design, and layout
© 2014 Quadrille Publishing Limited

ISBN 978-1-4547-0912-1

Distributed in Canada by
Sterling Publishing c/o Canadian
Manda Group, 664 Annette Street
Toronto, Ontario, Canada M6S 2C8

For information about custom editions, special
sales, and premium and corporate purchases,
please contact Sterling Special Sales at 800-805-
5489 or specialsales@sterlingpublishing.com.

Manufactured in China

10 9 8 7 6 5 4 3 2 1

larkcrafts.com

If you have any comments
or queries regarding the
instructions in this book,
please contact us at
LarkCrafts.com.